T0205185

"The Object Lessons s[...]
very close to magic: [...]
even banal—objects [...]
a rich history of invention, political struggle,
science, and popular mythology. Filled with
fascinating details and conveyed in sharp,
accessible prose, the books make the everyday
world come to life. Be warned: once you've read
a few of these, you'll start walking around your
house, picking up random objects, and musing
aloud: 'I wonder what the story is behind this
thing?'"

Steven Johnson, author of *Where Good Ideas
Come From* and *How We Got to Now*

"Object Lessons describe themselves as 'short,
beautiful books,' and to that, I'll say, amen. . . .
If you read enough Object Lessons books, you'll
fill your head with plenty of trivia to amaze and
annoy your friends and loved ones—caution
recommended on pontificating on the objects
surrounding you. More importantly, though . . .
they inspire us to take a second look at parts
of the everyday that we've taken for granted.
These are not so much lessons about the objects
themselves, but opportunities for self-reflection
and storytelling. They remind us that we are
surrounded by a wondrous world, as long as we
care to look."

John Warner, *The Chicago Tribune*

"For my money, Object Lessons is the most consistently interesting nonfiction book series in America."

Megan Volpert, *PopMatters*

"Besides being beautiful little hand-sized objects themselves, showcasing exceptional writing, the wonder of these books is that they exist at all. . . . Uniformly excellent, engaging, thought-provoking, and informative."

Jennifer Bort Yacovissi,
Washington Independent Review of Books

". . . edifying and entertaining . . . perfect for slipping in a pocket and pulling out when life is on hold."

Sarah Murdoch, *Toronto Star*

"[W]itty, thought-provoking, and poetic. . . . These little books are a page-flipper's dream."

John Timpane, *The Philadelphia Inquirer*

"Though short, at roughly 25,000 words apiece, these books are anything but slight."

Marina Benjamin, *New Statesman*

The joy of the series, of reading *Remote Control, Golf Ball, Driver's License, Drone, Silence, Glass, Refrigerator, Hotel,* and *Waste* . . . in quick succession, lies in encountering the various turns through which each of their authors has been put by his or her object. . . . The object predominates, sits squarely center stage, directs the action. The object decides the genre, the chronology, and the limits of the study. Accordingly, the author has to take her cue from the *thing* she chose or that chose her. The result is a wonderfully uneven series of books, each one a *thing* unto itself."

Julian Yates, *Los Angeles Review of Books*

The Object Lessons series has a beautifully simple premise. Each book or essay centers on a specific object. This can be mundane or unexpected, humorous or politically timely. Whatever the subject, these descriptions reveal the rich worlds hidden under the surface of things."

Christine Ro, *Book Riot*

. . . a sensibility somewhere between Roland Barthes and Wes Anderson."

Simon Reynolds, author of *Retromania: Pop Culture's Addiction to Its Own Past*

OBJECT LESSONS

A book series about the hidden lives of
ordinary things.

Series Editors:

Ian Bogost and Christopher Schaberg

Advisory Board:

Sara Ahmed, Jane Bennett, Jeffrey Jerome Cohen,
Johanna Drucker, Raiford Guins, Graham Harman,
renée hoogland, Pam Houston, Eileen Joy, Douglas
Kahn, Daniel Miller, Esther Milne, Timothy Morton,
Kathleen Stewart, Nigel Thrift, Rob Walker,
Michele White

In association with

BOOKS IN THE SERIES

fat

HANNE BLANK

BLOOMSBURY ACADEMIC
NEW YORK · LONDON · OXFORD · NEW DELHI · SYDNEY

BLOOMSBURY ACADEMIC
Bloomsbury Publishing Inc
1385 Broadway, New York, NY 10018, USA
50 Bedford Square, London, WC1B 3DP, UK

BLOOMSBURY, BLOOMSBURY ACADEMIC and the Diana logo are
trademarks of Bloomsbury Publishing Plc

First published in the United States of America 2020

Library of Congress Cataloging-in-Publication Data
Names: Blank, Hanne, author.
Title: Fat / Hanne Blank.
Description: New York, NY: Bloomsbury Academic, 2020. | Series: Object
lessons | Includes bibliographical references and index. | Summary:
"Fat combines the cultural imaginary about fat as object of fear,
pathology, and obsession with the material realities of fat as it
intersects with the human body"– Provided by publisher.
Identifiers: LCCN 2020029906 (print) | LCCN 2020029907 (ebook) |
ISBN 9781501333286 (paperback) | ISBN 9781501333293 (epub) |
ISBN 9781501333309 (pdf)
Subjects: LCSH: Fat–Social aspects. | Obesity–Social aspects. |
Body image–Social aspects.
Classification: LCC QP752.F3 B563 2020 (print) | LCC QP752.F3 (ebook) |
DDC 612.3/97–dc23
LC record available at https://lccn.loc.gov/2020029906
LC ebook record available at https://lccn.loc.gov/2020029907

ISBN: PB: 978-1-5013-3328-6
ePDF: 978-1-5013-3330-9
eBook: 978-1-5013-3329-3

Series: Object Lessons

Typeset by Deanta Global Publishing Services, Chennai, India
Printed and bound in the United States of America

To find out more about our authors and books visit www.bloomsbury.com
and sign up for our newsletters.

for Roxane Gay and Brittney Cooper

CONTENTS

FRONTISPIECE

"Ugh, I just feel so fat today," the woman near me in the locker room says to her friend as they get dressed after their workout. I look over—discreetly, as one does—to catch a glimpse of the grimacing side of her face as she zips up a pair of close-fitting blue jeans over a barely rounded lower abdomen, hip bones evident under taut fabric.

As I sit putting on my socks, I wonder whether this woman, who has just complained of feeling fat, has even registered that there is an actual fat woman not ten feet away. While she "feels fat" as she frowns her way into her formfitting tank top and comfortable, slouchy cashmere sweater, I can feel my ample belly pressing against my thighs and the oddly comforting, distinctly sensitizing way the elasticated wicking compression fabric of my gym top squeezes my fat back and belly and breasts from all directions at once. The garment is a variation on the theme of the sports bra: breasts are not the only body parts whose size varies in part because of the amount of fat they hold within their contours and are not the only body parts whose contrary motion can make high-impact exercise uncomfortable. I like the reassuring pressure of the compression fabric, and don't mind that it reminds me of parts of my body, like my fleshy mid back, that I don't think about too often unless they are being touched or, as they are now, comprehensively squished.

Locker-room etiquette demands that this woman and I will not make eye contact, nor will I acknowledge that she has spoken. Yet she and I are actually engaged in conversation. In our individual ways, we are taking two separate (and sometimes opposing) sides in a dialogue about fat that extends deep inside, but also far beyond, our own individual bodies and what may or may not be true about their composition. In the moment of our chance encounter, both of us were feeling fat, yet our experiences occupied no common ground whatsoever.

This is part of the nature of fat in the early twenty-first-century West. For us, fat has multiple personalities, multiple lives. As often as not, they seem, or at least are allowed to seem, to have little in common. Like any other material substance, fat can be seen, touched, sampled, studied, and, of course, weighed. In our bodies, as with mine in my athletic compression wear, it can be felt, stroked, hefted, caressed, squeezed, experienced as it moves with and within the body. Fat is an everyday thing, a bodily organ and a biochemical substance without which we would not be able to survive. It is as mundane and ubiquitous and as much a part of our nature as blood and bone. But you'd never know it by the way we talk about it, the obsession we have with getting rid of it, our conviction that it is inimical not just to a good life, but to life itself. As a lifelong fat woman, I am acutely aware that the fat I feel and experience every day both is and is not the fat we as a culture so obsessively think and talk about.

We compartmentalize fat. We like to imagine that the fat that keeps us going when we are too sick to eat is not necessarily the same as the fat that jiggles on our thighs. We do not like to think of the fat that makes us sexy—fat is central to the production of sex hormones, and famously rounds out breasts, hips, and butts—as being, y'know, *fat*. In any case, we tell ourselves, it's not related to the odious stuff we attribute with the ability to depress, stupefy, make repellent, desexualize, and even kill. In our imaginations fat is insidious as mildew, materializing mysteriously through mechanisms invisible, and as seemingly resistant to eradication as cockroaches. When George Lucas wanted a viscerally loathsome intergalactic gangster who could menace the heroes of *Star Wars: Return of the Jedi*, he created the slug-like—and enormously rotund, with hints of human chest and belly fat— Jabba the Hutt.

Yet without fat, there would be no *Star Wars* and indeed no George Lucas. Fat quite literally makes us possible. It gives our cells their membranes, helps us moderate our body temperature, enables us to reproduce. The human brain consists of approximately 60 percent fat. The protective myelin sheaths that insulate our nerves and axons have a similar composition. Without those fatty myelin sheaths, we would experience symptoms similar to those suffered by people with multiple sclerosis, the most common of the central nervous system demyelination disorders: loss of vision, weakness, numbness, nerve pain, brain lesions, tremors, cognitive and memory impairment, and much else. Without our fatty brains we could not, in the most literal of terms, think about fat. Even with them, we tend not to think about fat very clearly or very well. Fat has too many identities in our lives, too many meanings, and we are too reactive, too confused, and frankly, too ignorant.

Most of us are essentially unaware of fat as an object. We may not even know what fat is, strictly speaking. We have attached so much baggage to the word that it feels like an effort to think of fat as being just another word for a type of lipid that is solid at standard room temperature. We may or may not be able to clear out sufficient mental space to recall that lipids themselves are spontaneously occurring biological molecules whose most celebrated unifying characteristic is that they won't dissolve in water or other polar solvents. Fat is the reason that you have to shake your bottle of vinaigrette, creating a temporary suspension of lipids in vinegar, before you pour it on a salad. Fat is also one of the reasons that life first arose on this planet, scientists believe, the first cells organizing themselves within the protective shielding provided by micelles, tiny cages made of layered lipids. Fat is supremely useful and extraordinarily versatile. We generally don't think of things as diverse as linoleum, candles, soap, lipstick, and surfboard wax as having anything to do with fat, even though each of these are made of little else. Fat is everywhere.

Fat is everywhere, but we rarely see it. This sounds wrong on first hearing, but it is true. We rarely see fat itself. We may see it in the food we eat, like butter or the fat that renders in the roast chicken pan. We might observe it in the form of skin lotion or lip balm. But most of the time when we talk about "looking fat" our gaze is on bodies, and when we look at bodies, we do not see fat. What we see when we believe that we're looking at fat are places where fat has been deposited beneath the skin. Belly rolls, cellulite, love handles, thunder thighs—all are evidence of subcutaneous fat.

But they're not fat. The fat is where we cannot and do not see it: under the skin.

We find ourselves in the odd position of constantly seeing fat, constantly noting its presence, yet never actually seeing it at all. Most of us probably couldn't say what color human fat is. We might wonder whether it's all one color in any case. We might conjecture that like pork fat or beef fat tend to be when we encounter them on refrigerated cuts of meat, human fat must be cold and waxy, bloodless and hard. What would it look like if we could stick a hand into our own bodies and scoop some of our own fat out to look at it? Would it be wet or dry or greasy, lumpy or smooth or grainy? Does it get like butter, squishy-soft at room temperature or liquid at body temperature?

How much we presume to know, while hardly knowing anything at all! But this is of course how it works: the absence of knowledge of the object itself leaves a conveniently blank slate for projection, for fantasy, for symbol. In our imaginations, therefore, fat has a thousand faces. It can be our enemy, a public health threat, a personal failing, an outward and visible sign of inward moral disgrace. We might consider its very existence to be a pathology, a sickness, a thing to be cured. It can be hilarious and tragic, delectable and dangerous, monstrous and utterly, banally normal. What it means to us, how it makes us feel in any given context or moment, is more important than what it may be. In our heads, within the confines of our thoroughly fatty brains, we relentlessly imagine and indeed experience fat in a thousand ways that have only the most tenuous ties to its material reality. We have become mired in the disconnection, stuck in a way that feels perilous, unable to unstick ourselves without fearing the consequences of the movement it takes to get free.

In our daily lives and in research and scholarship as well, we are stuck in a set of fatty presumptions and projections. Biomedicine is only barely, and only grudgingly, capable of considering human body fat as anything but a crisis. For more than a century fat has been, in Louis Althusser's famous locution, "always already" a problem, an excess in the eyes of physicians whose learned ideologies of the body made it so. Where fat is seen, automatically and inevitably, as a pathology in need of comprehension, it becomes axiomatic that the point of comprehension is to solve the puzzle of the pathology, to acquire an understanding that leads at minimum to treatment and prevention, but also hopefully to eradication. This is one of the places that fat gets us stuck.

Another place we get stuck is when we presume that fat and obesity are one and the same. They are not. Fat is a substance. Obesity is a diagnostic term derived from the Latin word "obesus" by physicians for whom Latin was and is a symbol of elite learning and authority over knowledge. As all such diagnostic terms do, it isolates a thing, a state, a condition of the body as pathological, a thing that causes pathos, as the Greeks named suffering. Each time "obesity" is used synonymously or interchangeably with "fat," what it shows us is the always alreadyness of our beliefs about fat: that it cannot be anything other than inimical to happiness and human flourishing, an enemy to being healthy and well.

Unsurprisingly, academics outside of biomedicine also get stuck in the same places. Equally unsurprising, inherited ideas and their rhetorics offer two options: adoption or rejection. The discipline of fat studies arose, in part, out of the desire to reject the biomedical "always already" of fat as a source of suffering, to offer an alternative to the narrative that tells us that fat is never not troublesome. As such it is unavoidably reactive, in precisely the same ways elder sibling disciplines like critical race studies, women's and gender studies, queer theory, and disability studies tend to be. The work of chronicling, analyzing, and understanding marginalized embodiments is inherently a reaction against that marginalization. The laudable, valuable effort to reveal the workings of marginalization and power as they operate on and through human bodies begins, as it of course must, with being mired in a set of oppressive, often punitive, beliefs and assumptions from which there is no easy extrication. To dare to think that our bodies may not be built all wrong for this world, but that the world might be built all wrong for our bodies, thrills and exhilarates precisely as much as—and precisely because—it provides a way to get unstuck from the mire.

This book is an attempt to do something that might, if I am successful, offer a way to bypass the mire entirely. If anything at all has become obvious to me about fat in the twenty years that I've been writing and thinking about it, it is this: Fat is protean. It shifts its shape, manifests in multiple ways, exists on many levels. It is simultaneously a physical reality and a creation of the imagination. We approach fat presuming that we already know it and understand it. We use the word constantly, we denizens of the Western twenty-first century. We have exceptional confidence in our ownership of the concept, and in the rightness of our beliefs about it. We are so accustomed to dividing and compartmentalizing our thoughts about fat that we do not even notice that we are doing it. It seems simple enough. Fat is fat and that is that, and besides, why would anyone want to spend an entire book, however short, talking about it unless it was to tell us how to get rid of it?

Just so. Fat, and in particular human fat, deserves to be witnessed as the complicated thing that it is and has become. If I do my job right, this book will not make fat simpler or more limited; instead, it will multiply fat's meanings and possibilities exponentially. Fat might become bigger, more spacious, something that provides us freedom to think in new ways rather than continuing to be stuck in the same old mire.

1 FACT

Let us begin, then, by doing the thing we don't get to do, taking a good long look at the stuff we only think we're seeing when we see love handles or double chins or beer bellies. To consider fat this way is—as something literally more than skin deep and with a material existence of its own—a way of beginning to expand our thinking about fat. Human fat, like the fat of other mammals, is relatively solid at room temperature, a trait it owes to the long fatty acid molecules that make it up. Every fat molecule has a fatty acid attached to a glycerol molecule, and it is those fatty acids that make different kinds of fat so diverse. They affect the ways the molecules stack and how sturdily stacked the molecules are. Some will melt in the mouth or on the skin like the cocoa butter in chocolate, others require significant amounts of heat before the stacks of molecules slowly disintegrate into liquid. Lard, for example, is made through precisely that process: the white, layered fat that forms around the kidneys of pigs is cooked in order to render the pure fat out of the organic tissue. Heat turns the fat liquid, and the liquid can then be poured off and prepared for use. Allowed to sit in a dish at room temperature—which has been standardized at about 20° Celsius or 68° Fahrenheit—lard will solidify. Fats that go solid at room temperature are called "saturated" fats. Unsaturated fat molecules remain liquid. There are other classes of fats as well, like semi-saturated fats, hydrogenated fats, and trans fats, some of which occur spontaneously and others that are generated through manipulation of fat molecules, but they are less important for our purposes. We're here to talk about human fat, for the most part, and human fat is a saturated fat much like lard, solid at room temperature.

Like lard, much of human fat is white, or at least what is called "white fat." Often in humans it is not white but yellow, stained by the vivid beta carotenes we consume regularly via foods like carrots, red peppers, and winter squash. Fat exists in many colors, both inside the human body and outside it. We're familiar with the creamy hue of tallow, the greens and yellows of olive oil, the yellowy tan of beeswax, the red of palm oil. In humans, we add white (yellow), brown, and beige. Even at the level of color, the fat in our bodies is not all just one thing, one blob indistinguishable from the next. Not only do we contain multitudes, but so does our fat: white, brown, and beige fat each have distinctive identities and functions.

All forms of fat are part of the body's survival team. White fat's big job is to store energy in an easily available form. As a child, I recall being terrifically confused by this news: my mother's chilly loathing of fat had taught me only that fat was ugly, unwholesome, and unnecessary. Then one day a pediatrician, having weighed me and pinched my chubby little kid sides with a terrifyingly large cold set of calipers, lectured me at length about how fat existed only to store extra energy so a person wouldn't starve to death and, with a meaningful look over the tops of his eyeglasses, insisted I was clearly in no danger of starving to death. I knew perfectly well that squirrels got fatter before winter, having watched them feeding heavily under the oak trees in our Cleveland back yard, and I'd seen television documentaries in which bears fattened up for their long winter hibernation. Somehow I hadn't put two and two together and realized that fat did the same thing in people. The available glycogen in fat cells is easily transformed by the liver into glucose, the body's preferred fuel. Without glucose, cells literally stop functioning. Being deprived of glucose, for a cell, is just as bad as being deprived of oxygen. Take away a cell's supply of either or both and it dies. That, at the cellular level, is what starvation looks like. Body fat helps maintain the glucose supply not only in times of actual famine, as the depth of winter so often is for squirrels and bears and other creatures, but during all the times when we are too ill to eat, too busy or stressed to make time for lunch, or too poor to have enough to eat.

Protecting us from starving is white fat's primary job, but not its only one. It also releases hormones that help regulate metabolism, contributes to the protein-production process, insulates, and protects the skeleton and internal organs. A radiologist friend used to tell stories about her first internship weeks at a big Baltimore hospital, reviewing X-rays of people who'd been brought to the emergency ward with gunshot wounds. She often saw images without seeing the actual patients, and found herself sending out panicked reports about patients who had multiple bullets, broken-off tips of knife blades, and other startling and dangerous objects embedded in their bodies. The surgeons with whom my radiologist friend worked would laugh: they saw the actual patients, and knew from what they'd seen that they only had to worry about the bullets responsible for the raw, bloody, new entrance wounds they found. The rest could be safely left where they were, securely encased well beneath the skin, held by the patient's body fat. Metabolically, and in some cases materially, fat can be an excellent bodyguard.

It is an interestingly bloodless place, this white fat, but don't mistake bloodlessness for inertness. Most white fat is found under the skin, a subcutaneous layer of varying thickness. Although the skin itself is highly vascularized and contains myriad blood vessels and capillaries, veins and arteries, and the visceral body of muscles and organs is also chockablock with blood's tubes and tunnels, the fat that lies between them is not. The same is true of visceral fat, white fat that has been deposited deeper inside the body. Fat is surrounded by vascular tissue but doesn't often include it. White fat cells do not appear to require a lot of direct access to circulating blood. This is true despite the fact that fat cells are constantly productive, daily churning out supplies of substances that the body needs to function like estrogen, the inflammatory and insulin regulator called adiponectin, and a hormone called leptin that helps the body regulate its appetite for food. Lack of blood flow is no obstacle, nor does it keep fat cells from receiving all the chemical signals they need to do this job appropriately and in the right proportions. Even more impressive, white fat cells do all this without an internal energy source. Mitochondria, the subcellular organelles that generate chemical energy for almost all types of living cells, don't exist in white fat cells. It's one of the reasons they don't have a distinctive color of their own.

Brown fat, the body's other primary form of fat, does have mitochondria and is rich with blood vessels. Brown fat cells make their own energy and thus allow brown fat to contribute to our survival in a very different way, by generating heat. Babies have more of it, percentage wise, than anybody else for the simple reason that babies need the greatest amount of help regulating their own body temperature; we lose much of it as we grow to adulthood. As adults we have only a few ounces of the stuff, though women have a bit more than men and leaner people have a bit more than people with more white fat in their bodies. Whatever amount we may have, though, it is this brown fat that exists in the neck, between the shoulder blades, and in the spaces around the heart and kidneys, that lets our bodies keep the most vital vulnerable bits from getting cold. This thermogenic activity can only take place by using the energy contained in white fat. And this, of course, is of great interest to researchers who work on questions of how human beings might more intentionally regulate the amount of white fat in their bodies.

Sometimes, though not often, the body combines these two types of fat. "Beige Fat" has always sounded to me like a particularly good name for a punk band. In the body, it is exactly what it sounds like: a mix of white and brown fats that appears beige. Like brown fat, beige fat uses white fat cells to generate heat, and like white fat, beige fat stores glycogen for future use. We usually have even less of it than we do brown fat, located under the collarbone and along the spine. These few ounces of "specialty fats" are small but mighty, helping the body maintain the physical conditions it needs not only to survive but to thrive in this unpredictable world.

Beige fat tidily integrates all the aspects in which fat serves us as a survival mechanism. It seems competent in its multitasking way, efficient and helpful. But all fat does something useful, something the body needs, and something that only fat can do. This is why, when more food is taken in than the body can immediately use, it is stored against an unguessable, perhaps dangerous future. For every gram of fat metabolized—which is to say, converted back into usable glucose—the net gain in terms of energy from glucose is about 9 food calories, or to be a little more precise, 37 kilojoules. The availability of these grams of fat can be what makes the difference between life and death.

While we're on the subject, a few words about calories: a calorie has no innate relationship to fat. It is actually a measurement of heat energy, first introduced by the French physicist Nicolas Clément in 1824. A calorie, rather unglamorously, is merely the quantity of heat energy needed to raise the temperature of a precise quantity of water by one degree Celsius. Calories come in two sizes, based on the size of the quantity of water in question. "Small" calories function at the level of grams—how much heat energy it takes to raise the temperature of one gram of water by one degree Celsius—while the "large" calorie, standardized for use by nutritionists by American chemist Wilbur Olin Atwater in 1887, functions at the level of the kilogram. Measuring calories is a way of answering the following question for any given substance: Assuming standard atmospheric pressure, how much hotter could we make a kilogram of water using only the potential energy present in this substance? An Oreo cookie, for instance, could raise the temperature of a kilogram of water by about 53 degrees Celsius. It wouldn't be able to keep the water at that temperature, or make it any hotter. For that, you'd need more Oreos.

A calorie is not an object, not an item or a substance of which one eats either too many, too few, or possibly exactly the right amount. Search all you like, sift through every atom of your most recent meal, you won't find its calories anywhere. Not in cottage cheese, not in croissants, not in chocolate. This is true even though in theory anything that can be burned—a stick of firewood, a stack of old love letters—could be measured in terms of its caloric output, which is to say the heat it can generate. "Calories" is just another way of talking about the potential energy bound up within the molecules of a substance. Calories aren't things. The calorie is a concept, a unit of measure that allows us to quantify the potential energy bound up in the molecules of a substance.

Because the calorie is a unit of measure we could, if we liked, measure the energetic potential of a US gallon of gasoline (about 4 liters) is to say that it equates to about 31,000 calories. This is accurate, but it seems strange to think of it this way. This is because we have been taught since childhood not only to think of calories as things but as things that are specifically, and solely, found in food. Food "contains" calories, or so the nutrition labels that have been increasingly included in the packaging of prepared foods since 1973 (when the US Food and Drug Administration began to regulate them) have taught us to imagine, listing calories alongside other nutrients like protein, fiber, and vitamins. As a result we have come to think of calories as a representation of how "foody" a food is. "Low-calorie" foods are foods that, per unit of volume, do comparatively less of the central thing that food does: provide our bodies with energy. There are two ways to think about this. One is that low-calorie foods *require* us to eat a lot of them in order to obtain the energy we need, and therefore it's more difficult to obtain any useful excess. The other is that low-calorie foods *allow* us to eat a lot of them without obtaining all the energy we might need, thus lowering the chances that we will obtain any unwanted excess.

Which brings us back to fat. Human beings are not controlled environments. We are made of more than water, and our metabolic processes do not much resemble the excitingly named bomb calorimeters with which Atwater and others measured the energetic potential of foods. The reactions are far more complicated, to say nothing of the fact that we need much more from what we eat than just energy that can be turned into body heat. Cold-blooded creatures don't use their food energy to warm their bodies, after all, and as my anthropologist friend Keridwen Luis has been known to quip, "Even lizards have to eat."

It's been obvious for some time that in humans there is not a clear, one-to-one relationship between calories consumed and body weight. Yet in generating numbers to describe the energetic value of food, we have created the opportunity for a seductively simplistic belief about calories in versus calories out. It's a bit like thinking of the body as a bank: the more you put in and don't spend, the more you save (as fat) and the bigger your (fat) savings become. If you put in very little and spend a lot, your savings will dwindle. (Ironically for our late-capitalist culture, it's the one time we are encouraged, even bullied, to leave nothing whatsoever in the bank.)

This is true in large outline, but as ever, the devil is in the details. Unlike mechanical engines which have a fairly constant rate of energy utilization, bodies may need either more or less energy depending on environmental circumstances or internal body conditions. Also unlike mechanical engines, bodies can adjust, within limits, to a lack of food energy. As University of Minnesota researcher Ancel Keys discovered in his landmark 1945 experiment (generally known as the Minnesota Semi-Starvation Experiment), human bodies literally slow down and shrink the physical system so that the organism can survive with less energy. Keys's thirty-six volunteer subjects, many of them conscientious objectors who chose to participate in the starvation study rather than enlist in the Second World War, did not merely become alarmingly thin during the experiment's starvation phase, when they were being fed 1,570 calories daily; they also lost about ten percent of their normal blood volume as their body temperatures sank, their hearts shrank in size, and their heartbeats slowed. The mechanical equivalent would roughly be like having a car that, after its gas tank or battery had emptied, did not sputter to a stop and refuse to start again until fuel was added, but rather shrank its engine and ran more slowly for an indefinite (although not infinite) period of time.

But this was not the only lesson Keys's work, published in 1950 as *The Biology of Human Starvation*, had to teach us. Without sufficient energy in the form of food, human beings have trouble concentrating, lose interest in sex, and become depressed. Perhaps predictably, they also become preoccupied with food, a preoccupation that lasted long after the starvation phase of the experiment had ended, for Keys's volunteers. Keys also observed a curious phenomenon that has, like all his results, been multiply corroborated since the 1950s: semi-starvation neurosis. The experiment's subjects would spend hours nursing a single meal, even as their ability to concentrate on anything else evaporated. They became socially withdrawn, apathetic, and often neglected basic hygiene like brushing their teeth. The first time I read Keys's work, in my twenties, I did so in search of some insight about how to lose weight. What I found was a very different kind of insight: a very clear demonstration and explanation of why, every time I went on a diet, I ended up feeling cognitively and emotionally like something that had been scraped off the bottom of a shoe.

As Keys's study proved, human metabolism is both complex and dynamic, and importantly, the body's basal metabolic rate, or the amount of energy the body needs when at rest, declines when there is a consistent lack of available food energy. The body actually adjusts what it needs as best it can to align itself with what comes in. This is a genius move, when it comes to survival. It is also a vexing move for people whose attempts to lose weight are stymied by the body's ability to live on less. And this is not the only piece of the metabolic puzzle of fat. There is a considerable innate range of basal metabolic rates among humans. Our basic metabolic functions, such as keeping our bodies warm and oxygenated, building new cells, or removing waste products and other organic housekeeping, represent about 70 percent of our total energy use as humans. But how much energy, measured in calories, does that take? One study of 150 adults, performed by researchers at the University of Aberdeen, showed a range in basal metabolic rates from 1,027 calories per day all the way to 2,499 calories a day, a startlingly large variation. The researchers were able to account for about 75 percent of this discrepancy, which was largely attributable to body composition: lean body mass requires more energy to maintain than other types. Yet this still leaves us with what we might think of as 25-percent mystery. We simply don't yet know all the reasons that one person's body at rest might require literally one and a half times as much more energy than another's.

This is not the only way in which fat is a mystery. On the whole, fat is a fairly law-abiding organ in our bodies, a reasonably predictable substance. The reason we rarely hear about diseases like liposarcoma, a form of soft tissue cancer that begins, as the name suggests, among fat cells, is that they are both relatively rare and, as their rarity suggests, are not something caused by fatness or more likely to occur in fatter people. We do not know why about two people in a million will experience the condition, only that it's about twice as common in men and often occurs in areas of the body, like the neck, that we don't actually tend to associate with fat. What is clear is that neither overall body fat percentage nor calories in versus calories out are part of the puzzle of who will or won't get this kind of cancer.

The same is true of other major disorders of the organ and bodily substance that is fat. We live in a culture that would happily assign the blame for virtually any of the ills to which flesh is heir to our fatness, to our diets, even to specific numbers on scales. But our biomedical understanding of fat as an energy storage, as a hormone generator, as a regulator and messenger, provides far less certainty, particularly when we are faced with disorders of fat itself. The most commonly encountered disorders of fat, lipodystrophy and lipedema, are every bit as biomedically baffling as liposarcoma.

Lipodystrophy is a condition where the body loses fat—or it builds up in an unusual place—for no apparent reason. I remember well, during the early years of the HIV/AIDS epidemic, the way that friends living with AIDS would suddenly hit the point where they began to "waste away," their bodies shrinking and weakening horrifically, seemingly overnight. It was not until somewhat later that it would become evident that this lipodystrophy was part of HIV, and observably a side effect of some of the early antiretroviral drugs like protease inhibitors. Some of them would, paradoxically, accumulate fat in places like the back of the neck between the shoulders while their arms, legs, faces, and hips shrank into sharp boniness. Lipodystrophy, even less understood at the time than it is today, became part of the recognizable public face of AIDS. I recall sitting in a cloud of pot smoke with one sick friend, keeping him company while he tried in vain to induce a case of the marijuana munchies that might help him keep some weight on. It didn't work, but at least we were both high enough that we found it hilarious rather than disheartening.

Lipodystrophy can also occur congenitally, and in some cases is present at birth. Imagine expecting a chubby, healthy, round-cheeked infant, only to be handed a squalling little bundle of sunken cheeks, wiry muscle, and tiny, birdlike bones. In the condition known as Congenital Generalized Lipodystrophy (CGL), fat tissues are absent from birth, and no amount of carb loading will change it. Considered a rare but not usually fatal genetic disorder, the estimated worldwide prevalence is about one in 10,000,000. Lest this sound like an ideal state of affairs—imagine a body that would not become fat, no matter what you did or didn't eat or do—bear in mind that bodies that contain low or no fat are odd looking in their own way, bony, skeletal, and, without fat beneath the skin to provide youthful plumpness and fullness to the features, old looking. Lipodystrophies in general and CGL in particular also tend to be accompanied by an array of other health challenges ranging from the exquisitely painful and digestively disastrous condition known as pancreatitis to heart disease, atherosclerosis, steatosis and cirrhosis of the liver, enlarged spleen, infertility (particularly in people diagnosed female at birth), insulin resistance, and diabetes. Fantasize all you like about how wonderful it would be to never put on fat, but as they say, there's no such thing as a free lunch.

If there is a silver lining to lipodystrophy, I suppose it might be that it's the one medical condition that no one would blame on you being fat. This is not the case for the hundreds of thousands of mostly female-identifying people who suffer from lipedema and its near relative, Dercum's disease. In both of these conditions, subcutaneous fat accumulates disproportionately in certain parts of the body, most commonly from the hips to the ankles, sometimes with a distinctive difference in size between the lower leg and the foot. There is also often a distinct difference in size between the patient's upper body and their lower body, such that the upper body might seem average-sized or even thin, while the lower body is disproportionately fat. In Dercum's disease the fat appears initially in the form of lipomas, benign fatty growths, while in lipedema it initially appears to be more or less normal subcutaneous fat. What's different about these fat deposits, however, is that they are painful, even hypersensitive to touch, and the pain increases when the person engages in movement. Over time, connective tissue throughout these unusual and unusually large fat deposits becomes fibrous. There are a number of other related health problems that often accompany lipedema and Dercum's disease that range from joint issues to lymphatic system disorders. Both disorders have significant negative impact on patients' quality of life, and the chronic pain plus the physical abnormality of the condition are a blue-ribbon recipe for social isolation and depression.

The paradox of these disorders is that just as no one really knows why people with lipodystrophy lose their fat cells or simply cannot generate them, no one really knows why people with lipedema and Dercum's disease acquire fat cells in the numbers, sizes, and places that they do. Decades of research has shown that although some people who are ultimately diagnosed with lipedema or Dercum's are fat in a more generalized way, others are not. It has also shown that paradoxically, weight loss, whether through restricting food and increasing exercise or the more dramatic expedient of weight-loss surgery, has little to no effect on either lipedema or Dercum's.

Both are considered incurable and, indeed, difficult even to manage.

Yet many of the people who suffer from these conditions go years, even decades, without diagnoses. This happens almost entirely because doctors habitually dismiss patients who present with signs of these disorders, particularly in the early stages, seeing them simply as fat people who are in need of nothing more than some exercise and a diet. In fact, this is true across the board for many fat patients. "Obesity stigma," as the medical journals have taken to calling medical professionals' loathing and suspicion of fatness and fat people, frequently compromises medical treatment for fat patients, whose practitioners may spend almost a third less time with them than they do with thinner patients according to a 2019 review article in the *Journal of the American Medical Association*. Research published in 2010 in the *International Journal of Obesity* on medical interactions involving fat patients shows that fat patients may be as much as 40 percent more likely to be offered "diet and exercise" advice as treatment than thinner patients, and almost 20 percent less likely to receive the medications and therapies that physicians consider appropriate for thinner patients presenting with the same symptoms. Even in pediatric settings, according to a 2019 study in the *Journal of Clinical Psychology in Medical Settings*, the pain that fat patients suffer is significantly less likely to be acknowledged and taken seriously by health professionals.

Anecdotal reports of fat people with serious health problems being misdiagnosed or undiagnosed due to physicians' unwillingness to look beyond fatness as a cause of any symptoms are legion. Fat Canadian costume designer Ellen Maud Bennet's death in 2018 came just weeks after a very belated diagnosis with inoperable cancer, despite her having spent fruitless years seeking a diagnosis for her symptoms and being told to lose weight. I was saddened when I heard the news, but not particularly surprised. In my late twenties, I spent eight months experiencing excruciating right upper abdominal pain every time I ate. Because of the pain I ate little and infrequently, which led to a substantial weight loss that was sudden and disorienting, with frequent bouts of dizziness and vomiting. My then-doctor dismissed the pain as "probably lactose intolerance," praised me for the weight loss, and pretended to be shocked when I ended up on the operating table a few months later for emergency surgery to excise a pea-sized gallstone from my common bile duct and evict my miscreant gall bladder. Such stories, sadly, are not uncommon. Many of us who are fat try and fail to appease our doctors by losing weight when they insist that it is the source of our ills, only to discover that weight loss does not cure the underlying ailments that, as it turns out, have no causal relationship to our being fat.

This is inevitably the case for people with lipedema and Dercum's disease. When these people do lose weight, they discover that their lower bodies remain both fat and painful even as their faces grow gaunt and their clavicles protrude. Sometimes this is the point at which doctors finally realize that something unusual is going on and that something is decidedly wrong. People with lipodystrophy, lipedema, and Dercum's disease are the walking, talking counterarguments to the oversimplified claim that fatness is a simple matter of extraneous calories, of greedily consuming more than you'll use.

Despite the many situations where the supposed rule of calories in and calories out clearly does not apply, people will still wave their calorie tallies around and insist that you can't argue with the numbers. Except that they argue with the numbers anyway. Most of us do. There is a lot of bargaining, recitals of treats foregone and meals skipped and workouts logged in order to make it okay to order something other than a salad just this once. There is cellphone math, and muttering under the breath while someone mentally tabulates how many minutes of spin class will "burn off" the crème brulée or "just a tiny slice" of office birthday cake they ate that day. Sometimes, particularly in locker rooms, I hear the exasperation of a woman who has just stepped on the gym scale to discover that the latest privations and exertions have failed to move the needle, or worse, that some sadistic gremlin has nudged it in the wrong direction entirely. I have done it myself. For several years in my twenties I went through life clutching little spiral-bound notebooks in which I dutifully inscribed columns of calories consumed and those theoretically "burned off" through exercise. Those notebooks and the endless marching columns of numbers in them did not, and indeed could not, tell me why it was when I ran my hands over my naked body in the shower or in bed at night, what I felt was always, and apparently was always going to be, fat.

These arguments are not unusual. They are part of the scenery of modern life, annoyingly common as fat itself. Our arguments of addition and subtraction are merely a part of the soundtrack that accompanies our dreams of perfectible, predictable bodies that behave how we want them to, that respond to our prompting, our exercise, our food restriction in predictable, reliable ways. We insist, with a hope that is almost touching considering the vast contradictions of experience, that it's just a matter of doing things correctly, getting all the numbers right.

In our scientific, relentlessly mechanized world, we have been taught to put our trust in numbers, in mathematics and their sister sciences. This has been true since the nineteenth century and the first dreamlike imaginings of the standardized body, the "normal" citizen. This was, for the record, a European dream at first. The intellectual seductiveness of the "normal" body first emerged through the work of a statistician named Adolphe Quetelet, a Belgian who gave us the concept of the "average man" as a common denominator, the physical parameters of the desirably built body of the healthy and more importantly productive citizen. His work, published in 1845 as *Sur l'homme et le développement de ses facultés, essai d'une physique sociale*, arrived at precisely the right moment to influence the thinking of industrialists everywhere. What if the dimensions of things could be standardized? What if, instead of making each shirt collar and shoe for its particular wearer, carefully fitted to the peculiarities of that body and its contours, these things could simply be made in average sizes for average humans? What if the looms and engines that wove the cloth and spun the thread were simply built in whatever size was average, and the bodies that worked with those machines day after long, arduous day could be made to conform to the machines rather than the other way around? Imagine the savings of not having to build or alter machines to fit individual workers! Imagine the economies of scale possible when salable commodities could be churned out by the impersonal, averagely proportioned thousands at a time and not the individually crafted, made-to-measure few!

There would, of course, be deviants. "Deviations" is of course the correct word, when we speak of statistics and averages, but in the case of bodies the two are often conflated into one. When we began to imagine, as a culture, that part of being a good citizen lay in having proper size and shape and proportion, we placed another heavy layer of expectations on the body and the self. Imagining the physically disabled and the congenitally unusually shaped as deviant was nothing new, of course. Human "monsters and prodigies," as fourteenth-century physician Ambroise Paré titled his catalogue of birth defects, had been around as long as humans themselves, amazing and often frightening those who saw them. Now, though, what constituted a "deviant" body began to change. As the spectrum of "normal" shrank to that of statistical averages, the spectrum of "deviant" grew to include all who did not fit, or perhaps more to the point, all who could not be forced into, those "average" molds.

The nineteenth century was a time of extraordinary scientific and medical advancement, the era of the telegraph and typewriter, surgical anesthesia and germ theory, the machine gun and the first ever isolated virus. The physical world was becoming more known and knowable and at the same time, more amenable to being manipulated to our desires. This included our own human bodies, whose mysterious inner workings seemed to be yielding themselves up one by one to the overwhelming authority of science. While *Frankenstein* is the infamous morality tale of the era (as its subtitle "The Modern Prometheus" hints) this burgeoning idea that applied science could and should be able to control bodies and the workings of life itself began to shape many human lives, too.

Sometimes it also ruined them. The story of Robert Schumann is, if you'll pardon the pun, a note-perfect cautionary tale for the era. Schumann, a composer and pianist in his twenties, fell victim to the desire to alter his body to better suit the piano, the machine that was the center of his life's work. According to the papers of his piano teacher and mentor Josef Wieck— incidentally also the father of the famous concert pianist Clara Wieck, who later became Schumann's wife—the young Schumann permanently injured his right hand through the use of a (possibly homemade) finger-strengthening machine. One such machine, commercially made and sold under the name "Dactylion," featured rings for each finger connected to flexible metal brackets that projected from an apparatus worn around the wrist, forcing the wearer to press the fingers down with great force to flex the metal brackets enough that the fingers could press the piano keys. Logic seemed to insist that this would create muscular, powerful fingers, strong enough to wring the entirety of the possible dynamic range out of an instrument whose volume depended on how hard the keys were struck.

Schumann's concert pianist career was over before it had begun, fingers permanently cramped by his Dactylion-like device. This was probably not the first time someone was maimed in the attempt to perfect the body or to force the body to change to better fit the constraints of something that had been built with an idealized body in mind; it most certainly would not be the last. I have always thought it a particularly telling story, though. Schumann did not subject himself to the awkward and no doubt painful finger strengthener because he was forced to. Rather, he did it out of ambition and desire, the yearning to be not merely a great pianist but a superlative one, the object of everyone's praise and admiration including his concert-pianist love's.

Such fantasies of perfecting the body in the way that one might perfect a machine, by tinkering with its parts and proportions and applying external pressures and guides, was one of the core fantasies of the age. It is still with us. As the idea of a "standard" body gained ground and the notion that bodies could be regulated to meet those standards followed, the good citizen became the "average" citizen who was the citizen whose body and bodily capacities fitted the things that were made with the "normal" body in mind. The world's demands on the body were becoming ever clearer and more stringent. What the body might need from the world was less often considered, let alone considered a valid question.

Little wonder that we have, over the decades, learned to equate our feelings (and even our fears) of being unaccommodated, unacceptable, or unincluded with being fat. How could we fail to associate fatness with the specter, as well as the reality, of not fitting in, of being "too much" for the society in which we live? Bodies that refuse to play along with the numbers games of "average" and "typical" seem intransigent in their emphatic failure to be what our ideology tells us they should be. "Feeling fat" need have nothing to do with feeling or being fat, only with feeling somehow very wrong. Feel fat, bad citizen! Feel fat, deviant! Feel fat, misfit! That is where this feeling, this emotion lies, not in hands pulling compression fabric up over a heavy belly and thick hips, not in the numbers on the scale that can do nothing but express a quantitative statement of one's relationship to gravity. The willful animal body, even should it briefly conform, is never far from threatening our always imperiled social self. Little wonder we've learned to loathe it, and to blame so much on it. Little wonder we work so hard to bend it to our will.

2 FRIEND

Late at night, I sometimes wake up to the sensation of my husband's hand on my side near my armpit. You might think, as I did when he first began to do it, that he was working on slyly copping a feel, sliding his hand over my side to my breast. But no, his hand remains where it is, fingers cupping, then gently kneading, a bit of flesh I never imagined had any redeeming value, let alone be something a person could love. There, just below my armpit, he finds a handful of something that has no real name, though some might refer to it as "sideboob."

On my body, the sideboob is squishy and yielding, the skin delicate and so very soft. A frequent insomniac, my husband finds this handful of flesh deeply restful, comforting on a visceral level. Years ago, as he recovered from a complicated and painful surgery, kneading this bit of my body was one of the only things that helped him sleep at all. Sometimes he reaches for it when he is dead asleep, his unconscious mind very clear about what it wants for comfort.

At one point in my life I would have thought of this bit of my body as pointless, an ugly redundancy of flesh, unacceptable and unlovable, a thing to wish away, diet away, and hide. Now I am glad of it, and glad of my husband's unselfconscious pleasure and comfort in it, because every time I feel his hand on my side groping for his favorite spot in the night, I smile to think that my fat can be such a kind friend.

This is not, I'm well aware, a common way to feel about fat. In our current fat-loathing culture it is rare to go an entire day without encountering some manifestation of the message that fat is something we are supposed to loathe, abominate, and above all else, avoid. More than once I have had thin people inform me (as have several of my fat friends) that they'd rather kill themselves than be fat like me. (I confess, when confronted with this level of cruel self-righteousness I've been tempted to retort "Why wait?") There is copious research documenting the manifold ways in which fat is loathed, feared, hated, and an even more copious array of works reinforcing those notions as being only right and proper. The reader may avail themselves of that literature if they like; it is neither summarized nor imitated here.

Fat is a friend. I don't mean merely biologically, although of course it's true that fat does many things for us that nothing else can or does. Like water and protein, it is one of the basic macronutrients that we consume for our survival. Without fat, the much-ballyhooed big wrinkly brains that make us so different from our fellow animals would falter; we'd have a hard time focusing and remembering. Recent research at Massachusetts General Hospital for Children on female athletes experiencing amenorrhea showed that very low body fat and consequent low estrogen compromises not just reproductive capacity—hence the lack of menstrual periods—but also cognitive abilities. Perhaps we shouldn't be surprised by this, since this is one of the reasons chubby babies tend to be healthy babies. Babies optimally go from about 10 percent body fat at birth to 25 percent by their first birthday in part to help ensure the smooth, uninterrupted development of a brain that must grow from about one quarter of its adult size to 80 percent in just two years. The high fat content of human breast milk, about half of which is fat, helps. But only babies who get extra milk, not the mere minimum that their little bodies require, are able to store the excess energy in the form of body fat that ensures an uninterrupted, metabolically well-supported growth process for both body and brain.

From the very beginning, both bodily and dietary fat are built into who and what we are, how we function, and whether we succeed in life. Take them away and we have a hard time staying warm and our hormones get out of whack, our fertility plummets, our bones grow weaker, and our skin roughens. Fat, paradoxically for something that many assume to be so deadly, actually helps our bodies to fight infection. In its absence we are not only more likely to get sick, but when we do we are more likely to die due to lack of energetic reserves to deploy in the fight. Without fat in our bodies or our diets we'd be weak and without stamina. By and by our hearts would slow, possibly to the point of stopping altogether. The heart may or may not give out first, however, given that without a sufficient and stable source of energy the brain will also slow to a halt, causing lack of consciousness followed by seizure, coma, and eventually death. That is what it means to starve to death.

But this is the easy part. Even in our fat-loathing society we are willing, however grudgingly, to make allowances for the biologically necessary. It's far harder for us to acknowledge that fat might be worth befriending for other reasons, that perhaps there are compensations, benefits, even delights to be found in fat. And no, I don't just mean tits and ass, though those certainly qualify. Having been fat, to some degree or another, for as long as I can remember, fat and I have a longer relationship than I have had with any other entity. This is not to say that it is an uncomplicated relationship, that we have never fought, or that I've never considered what my life would be like if I could jettison this entity altogether and experience something entirely different. (Let us not delude ourselves about the nature of long, intimate relationships!) It is also not in any way to suggest that my relationship with fat is everyone's relationship with fat, that others have the same experiences or understandings, or that they should. Indeed, the diversity of fat experiences and manifestations are among the reasons I consider it a friend.

If we so much as glance in its direction, fat reminds us, tangibly and insistently, of human variety. Cartoons of fat bodies tend to make all fat bodies look the same, weirdly buoyant as if they've been inflated with helium. "Headless fattie" images in the media, those floating depersonalized round torsos who've had their heads chopped off for their sins, have a similarly homogenizing effect. But the reality of fat bodies is different. It has been my good luck and my pleasure to spend some time in spaces populated exclusively by fat women, at pool parties and clothing swaps, spas and hot springs. The sheer variety of fat bodies never ceases to impress me. Every quirk and variation of proportion and size is magnified when fat is added and the body becomes bigger, the individuality of the body more pronounced with varied lines and proportions. All the variegated possibility of human form is there, writ in all different sizes and gradations of large: bellies and butts, sure, but also calves and backs and arms, breasts large and small, hips and thighs. The landscapes undulate and curve, the hills rise and fall in different places, at different rates. There are bodies shaped like cellos and bodies that might've just stepped out of Rubens paintings. There are Venuses of Willendorf and there are bodies as elegantly round and self-contained as eggs. They move differently, some firm, some loose, some jiggling, some swaying, circles and ovals and mounds and rolls. Fat bodies make their variety instantly appreciable to those with the eyes, and the bravery, to actually look at their differences.

I did not always have the eyes to see all of this variety or to appreciate what I saw. I had to learn to savor bodily difference. But the experience of living in a fat body helped me learn. Being in the world, for a fat person, can be isolating and strange and stressful. One's physical self is often inadequately accommodated, one's bodily characteristics unaccounted for and unrepresented. Schoolroom desks don't fit right, let alone gym uniforms; one learns rapidly that the flimsy sidewalk café chair must be evaluated with a jaundiced eye, the ungainly mangle of the turnstile cannily negotiated, the airline seat belts assessed to see whether there's a need to flag down one of the flight crew for an extender that can be handed rather obviously to you after it is used to demonstrate how the buckles work. One quickly learns that the corpulent will be summarily bounced from any amusement-park ride for which they are even a bit over the weight limit, and that there is no sympathy to be had for it.

If your body is wrong enough that you cannot literally fit in, it's your problem. So is the stress of constantly having to negotiate a narrow world and its attitudes toward your wide body. The allostatic load—by which we mean the day-to-day environmental demands that are placed on an individual creature—can turn into allostatic overload when there is constant, unavoidable stress. Allostatic overload, in turn, leads to all the ills to which the overstressed human body is heir: heart problems, sustained high blood sugar, high cholesterol with low levels of high-density lipoprotein (HDL or "good cholesterol"), atherosclerosis, and, surprise surprise, depositing more than normal amounts of fat. Constant unavoidable stress is part and parcel of having a body that does not fit in. The culture of the "average" body exists, in part, as a disciplinary device. It is neither accidental or coincidental that it excludes people, or that those who are excluded suffer as a result. This suffering is compounded by the body's silent but significant attempts to cope with being constantly subjected to stress.

As a young child I had already learned through experience that sometimes my fatness would mean I was excluded from things or would feel left out.

It stung, of course. And yet where some children might've done anything they could to change, to fix whatever it was so that they could fit in, my response was to look for other excludees. I'm not sure why, but it was where my intuition led, the start of a lifetime of deep and careful engagement with the ways bodies and selves collide—on the margins, in the center, in public and in secret—with the cultures in which they live.

I watched for fat people on the street, at the library, on the television, looking for someone who looked like me, who was shaped like me, eyes wide for a little solidarity, a little possibility. I treasured the fact that my pediatrician was fat, that my beloved sixth-grade teacher and grammar-school music teacher were, too. It meant something, in a world where I was reminded constantly that I was wrongly shaped, wrongly sized, wrongly composed of the wrong stuff, to see people who looked like me in important positions in the world. They were recognized, they had power. They treated me well, and taught me well, and I loved them. More importantly, they cared for me, took care of me, and praised me when I did well—thus they were, in my young eyes, radiantly beautiful.

There were impressively successful fat people in the other major part of my young life as well. From the age of seven until I was in my early thirties, I sang professionally. The proverbial fat lady singing was, and remains, a joke. Legendary fat singers are simultaneously worshipped as divas and regularly ridiculed with nicknames like "Just Enormous" (Jessye Norman) or "Monsterfat Cowbelly" (Montserrat Caballé). The opera world's deep ambivalence about fat bodies breeds both ferocious pressure for singers to be thin and, simultaneously, a pragmatic understanding that voices arrive in bodies that may or may not be camera ready, idealizably gorgeous, and slim.

Dramas about size and gender and power play out in different ways on the operatic stage than they do on the ground. In our daily lives we are told from childhood that women should be, even that they have a responsibility to be, small and thin. We should be willing, at all times, to make ourselves smaller and make room for men. Male dominance includes rules about space and who has a right to it: watch who gets out of whose way on a busy sidewalk, a crowded workplace hallway, a rush-hour train. Women generally speaking and fat women particularly are taught from childhood to make themselves small for the sake of others' comfort. Not their physical comfort, mind you; women will clasp their hands in front of themselves, hang back, and make space for men even when there is already adequate space. Women's willingness to make themselves smaller is about psychic comfort: men's comfort in terms of always having space and always having space made for them, and everyone's comfort in terms of knowing that women are obeying the rules and doing what they're supposed to.

For fat women there is yet another layer to this imperative to shrink and yield. Our bodies, being unacceptable, should be minimized even more. If not literally, then through the apologetic body language of slouching, slumping, wearing loose clothing that does not call attention to itself, not making eye contact, and, of course, making sure that we do not attempt to put ourselves or our bodies on display. Like most fat women, I was raised to do this, and as a young woman did so. But opera intervened.

On the opera stage, the body is the vehicle for the voice. Preferences for thinner bodies, smaller bodies, conventionally beautiful bodies, simply cannot always be met: a glorious voice shows up in whatever body it shows up in. This was the moral of Susan Boyle's stunning 2008 success on *Britain's Got Talent*, when a cynical audience reacted with utter shock at the dumpy, fat, unbecomingly permed Boyle's stunning voice. For the right voice, opera—and its ancillaries, like the pop-classical realm in which Boyle performs— simply makes it work. Sometimes it seems ridiculous, for instance when a fat Mimi dies of consumption, or a corpulent Salome must wriggle her way through the Dance of the Seven Veils. But if the voice is enough, it is enough. All the rules can be broken. Fat women, and fat men as well, can stand center stage, dressed in dazzling costume, the spotlight trained on their bodies and faces.

In this line of work, the fat body is perhaps second best, but not out of the question. Opera singers, thin and fat, are trained to be visible, to be physically imposing, to take the stage and hold the audience. One dare not be physically apologetic. That rule, so reflexive everywhere else, cannot apply on stage. I vividly remember a conservatory opera director screaming and gesticulating at me from the third row in rehearsal, his face livid with exasperation. "Oh for Heaven's sake! It doesn't matter if you're huge, the audience paid to see you! Sail when you move! SAIL! Like an ocean liner, for God's sake! You're the *Queen Mary*, not a fucking rowboat!"

I was shocked to be called out, mortified to be likened to both a dinky little rowboat and an enormous, ponderous ocean liner. *I am ridiculous*, I remember thinking, *the proverbial fat lady, singing.* All I was missing were the Wagnerian spear, breastplate, and horned helmet; otherwise I was in every way the cliché. But I did what the director said and for the first time in my life, intentionally and unapologetically occupied every cubic inch of my fat body. As I moved across the stage, I could feel the difference, the easy expansion of my chest and swing of my arms when I was not trying to constrain or hide a round torso, the authority of my stride when I walked as if I knew the world would clear a path for me. I could not have put it into words at the time, but what I learned from that screaming director was vital: fat was not in itself ignominious. It mattered how I wore it.

Opera taught me to welcome being seen and taking up space and showed me just how important it was not to cede. I learned rapidly that in most circumstances, if I moved and stood with unapologetic authority, people would simply give it to me. The less afraid I became of not making the usual wordless apologies for my body, the more comfortable I grew with the knowledge that my fat body could intimidate, impose, and insist. In fact, as I rapidly apprehended, it could even do things fat bodies were not supposed to be able to do at all: seduce, enchant, and dazzle.

To thrive in an unaccommodated, dispossessed, denigrated body requires this, a well-cultivated, sometimes stubborn, knowledge of its worth. When I now call fat a friend, some may think I am merely engaging in apologetics and sophistry, making a flimsy plea for the rightness of something inherently wrong. I am not. When I call fat a friend, I mean it. I could even call it a mentor.

Outliers have no choice but to cultivate perspective. There's no way to survive without it, without figuring out what the unspoken rules are, without a keen knowledge of precisely the things and people that define the center and push you out of it. Those in the center rarely bother to look toward the peripheries with an investment in understanding them, only with the goal of measuring the distance between so that they can reassure themselves that there is some. The result is the spiteful, jealously kept fragility of thinness, of whiteness, of masculinity, of heterosexuality, of able-bodiedness, of wealth. All, when damaged, spew shards outward, toward the periphery. You learn how to stay out of the way. But you perhaps also learn something else: that when somebody is afraid of some aspect of you, or ashamed, or otherwise upset enough that they push that thing away hard and fast . . . there is power there. Knowing that is vital. Once you realize that there is power in that collision, you begin asking a different question: who gets to use it and to what end?

What a valuable question it turns out to be. Not because of its answer, which is of course that it varies, but because of the realization that this is, in fact, always a live question. Famously, this is not a thought that the marginalized, enslaved, and oppressed are encouraged to entertain, for it is the beginning of resilience composed of more than scar tissue and self-knowledge that goes far beyond what one is taught to parrot. Volatile, dangerous stuff. Just being around it sharpens the wits and the senses. What, indeed, would it mean to be able to use the power inherent in your own physical nature, and to use it to your own ends just as those at the center do? Liberation is always both a threat and a promise. But to consider it means considering that there is something, someone there, that might deserve to be free. This changes the world.

Fat got me to that question. This is not to say that it gets everyone there, or that everyone who does get there does the same thing once they do. But I know that I am not the only one who got to that crucial stage of self-awareness and self-value because of fat, and the experiences of being fat and living in a fat body. However difficult it can be to live with this knowledge of the world and the self—as everyone who has ever been in psychotherapy knows, insight sometimes feels like a booby prize—it is also an enormous gift. I have fat to thank for that, and for the ways this gave me a foundation on which to build a life. If that is not worth celebrating and cherishing, I am not sure I know what would be.

As a result, I am unashamed to say that I find fat to be much more often a comfort than a source of any kind of distress. I have occasionally been asked whether, given the chance to take a pill that would effortlessly turn me thin, I would take it. For years I didn't know how to answer and felt strange about my hesitation. It was precisely what I was supposed to want, what everybody is supposed to want. Who would not, all things considered, want to instantly and painlessly attain a body guaranteed to be acceptable, fashionable, loveable? Me, apparently. I have my reasons.

One of the things that being fat has done for me is make me very sensitive to the fact that when it comes to bodies, acceptability and certainly fashionableness are hardly absolutes. All my life I have listened to other people, especially women, bemoan physical shortcomings invisible to my eyes, and struggled to understand it. I briefly dated a woman who was solidly convinced that her ankles were her only redeeming physical feature. Much to the detriment of our relationship, it was a conviction my bountiful enthusiasm for the rest of her could not seem even to begin to overturn. She was not the only woman I have watched tear herself apart daily, hourly, sometimes minute-by-minute for her supposed physical flaws. I once sat clutching my mug of tea, pulling tissue after tissue out of my handbag as the woman across the table from me, a conventionally gorgeous woman, tall and long limbed with glorious auburn waves covering her shoulders like a cloak, wept about her inability to let her husband touch her or see her naked lest he see or touch a part of her she perceived as fat. How fascinating, how horrid it was to sit there as an unequivocally fat woman with a robust and fun sex life and realize that there was absolutely nothing I could say and no way in which my own example would convince her that something else might be possible for her. She had very little discernable fat but found even the thought of it so horrific that her imagination betrayed her, telling her that the only possible reaction to her body was disgust.

This is not an uncommon betrayal, as thousands of people intimately know. We live in a culture that deliberately constrains our ability to imagine good, valuable bodies and selves. Once I began to imagine that, and even more than that, I found myself unable to imagine less again. I discovered that the "Would you take the magic pill?" question was only a question, one that did not collapse instantly into a relieved yes but one that remained open. Now, when someone asks me that question I tend to answer with another question: I dunno. Do I get to change back?

I have wondered what it might be like to live in a very different and less fat body, in the same way that I occasionally wonder what it would be like to be a man and go through life with weirdly vulnerable dangly bits protruding from my crotch. I've mused about what it would be like to have certain types of physical interactions be basically effortless, for instance, being able to walk into a department store and find some fashionable clothing that fit tolerably well. It sounds fun, and freeing, in a similar way to the idea of sitting back, in the quintessential mode of entitled males, and letting other people work to please you. But neither are things I require, and I am a bit suspicious of them both. Being instantaneously thin would be a fun experiment, and then, I suspect, I would want to change back. It's fun to have adventures, but part of the fun of adventuring is returning home, where you can be at ease among friends.

3 FOE

Fat, we are emphatically taught and reminded daily in American culture, is ugly, disreputable, and dangerous. It is a killer, the agent of heart attack, high blood pressure, diabetes, stroke. It is evidence of poor self-discipline, proof of irresponsibility for one's own health and that of the nation. It indicates greed and monstrous self-indulgence and thus betrays not only a lack of morals but, or so our culture insists, also a lack of intelligence and self-regulation. Small children, sensibly enough, learn early on how to interpret and mimic adult expressions of dislike and disgust, and so they begin early to make the connection between seeing fat and expressing revulsion. Fat is not innately repulsive. If it were, our healthy chubby babies would never survive the rejection. The point is that we are taught to believe that it is.

My purpose in writing this chapter is not to stipulate that all the things we are taught to believe about fat's dangers and downfalls are incorrect, nor to assert that they are. Instead, it seems important to me to take some time to consider this idea that fat is a foe, a consistent and ubiquitous threat. We react to fat with such strength—of emotion, of conviction— that it would be disingenuous not to wonder why. It is virtually impossible to exist in the present-day United States and be unaware that fat is broadly considered to be one of life's most serious problems, a thing to be avoided at all costs; at the same time we know, and deeply resent, that fat is always already with us. We cannot avoid letting it in because it was there from the very beginning. How fascinating, then, that we condemn it out of hand. We have always been at war with Eastasia.

The war metaphor, and the Orwellian invocation, are not in the least hyperbolic. We are daily encouraged to think of ourselves as being at war with fat. We fight "the battle of the bulge," equip ourselves with an array of so-called "fat blasters." We pay money to guns for hire who tell us they know how to strategize our approaches and direct our campaigns. In this war, as in every war, psychology matters. Hating and fearing the enemy enough to fight it is key. A foe like fat (which seems so insidious and wily and continually "defeats" our best efforts to eradicate it although it does not fight, or fight back, at all) requires that we continually stoke the vigor and intensity of our loathing. Especially in the absence of decisive victory, we must strive to keep morale high.

We have not always done this, as a culture. Western culture does not, history reveals, have an intrinsic conflict with fat. We have always noticed it, if the historical record may be trusted and literature serve as a guide. But it has not always been seen as the immortal enemy it is today, and this tells us a few important things. First, it tells us that our present war against fat had a beginning, and as with all wars, there were reasons it started and a time when it began. In this case, the backstory is not simple. There are two intertwining histories, one basically biomedical and the other social, that explain how we got onto this fatty field of battle. Here I must beg your indulgence as a historian: these are not cleanly chronological tales, one picking up where the other leaves off. Think of them instead as rhizomes, invisible roots spreading and tangling out of sight. The growth we do not see is vaster and more important than the sprouts that rise to the surface, and it takes a little digging to see where the connections lie.

The term "obesity," derived from the Latin word *obesus*, does not show up in medical literature until 1622. Prior to the nineteenth century, the medical conversation about fat was fairly small potatoes. Fat was not an unknown thing, of course, but neither was it something that occupied many physicians' time or energy. There was no war, no frantic expenditure of energy and expertise, no sense of urgency whatsoever when it came to fat. Across most of the historical medical literature, fat is as essentially neutral as any other element of the body. It could, perhaps, be the site of trouble. But it was more likely not to be.

Some might wonder whether this lack of medical urgency about fat was due to ignorance—of what we assume must've been the insufficient knowledge of those who lived long ago. The answer is no. The past may be another country, as the saying goes, but its residents were not necessarily less smart or capable than we. Our ancestral physicians were observant. They did recognize that in some cases, fat might presage or accompany health problems. The Persian physicians of the so-called "Middle Ages" are our best resource not only for their own approaches to health and the body but for their encyclopedic knowledge of the Greek and Roman medical corpus, which they preserved through a period where we supposedly more civilized Westerners tended to let our classical inheritance rot. These Persians, like Al Rhazi and Ibn Sina and Ibn el Nefiz, wrote between the ninth and thirteenth centuries, and they associated excessive fatness with a number of health conditions; they connected it with some of what we'd now call endocrine disorders, for instance. They also observed that fatness sometimes seemed connected, although they were not sure how, to vascular accidents that we would now call heart attacks or strokes.

But even as these learned professionals agreed that excessive fatness might be medically troublesome, their conversation about it was also vague. They didn't define how much fat was "excessive" or risky. They disagreed about what caused fatness, as well. Sometimes doctors considered it congenital, others blamed it on imbalanced humors. It might be a result of wrong diet, or caused by too little mental activity, or too much of the wrong kind of thinking. It could be caused by some combination of these, or, depending on the case and the physician analyzing it, by something else entirely. Treatments, such as they were, were correspondingly varied and probably of variable effect. We don't know for certain, though, because these past physicians did not spill any ink on it, suggesting that they didn't see it as a major worry. And as improbable as it seems to us today, this makes sense. Fat is not going to be the biggest of any doctor's worries in an environment where people regularly die, as our ancestors routinely did, in childbirth, of infections, of mysterious epidemics, of diarrhea. If a person was healthy enough and sufficiently well fed to be fat, they were probably doing pretty well.

In the largely Christian West, at the same time, fat had come under a different kind of scrutiny. Since the earliest centuries of Christianity, the body and its appetites were considered suspect at best and villainous at worst. Food, drink, sex, and all sensory pleasures distracted the believer from prioritizing their relationship with God. Furthermore, they presented an obstacle to maintaining a body that could be a pure enough vessel for God to dwell within it. The Church soon developed a calendar of fast days, as well as the occasional feast, in order to regularize the process. Repudiating the flesh by refusing food became a recognized part of building virtue, a pattern Rudolf Bell and other historians, including Caroline Walker Bynum and Joan Brumberg, have dissected at length. For women believers in particular, who lacked the more public and heroic options through which men could prove their purity of heart and devotion, the result could be a condition similar in some ways to what we now call anorexia nervosa. *Anorexia mirabilis*, as this religiously motivated refusal to eat has been called, was simultaneously viewed as extreme, dangerous, and sufficiently holy that it is highlighted in the hagiographies of saints. Catherine of Siena, who died in 1380 at age 33 after defying her superiors' orders that she eat more than just the daily Eucharist, was only one of many holy women for whom the Church's calendar of consecrated fasts were never enough.

Over time, through the recognition of the holiness of fasting and the sacredness of purifying the human vessel, thinness became a recognized sign of virtue and fat became synonymous with sinful indulgence.

It is no accident that Lent, the season of fasting, mourning, and penitence that leads up to Easter, is customarily preceded by a festival of indulgence. "Mardi Gras" or "Fat Tuesday" is a reference to all the fatty foods that are forbidden during Lent. "Carnival" comes from the Latin *carne vale*, to put away meat, as is done during Lenten observance. During the apex of the liturgical year's reenactment of the life of Christ, the moment most tightly tied to sacrifice and redemption, Church doctrine demands that even the most lowly of believers restrict their food to literally meager—the word derives from the Latin *macrum*, meaning skinny or emaciated—fare. Virtue and thinness, holiness and fasting, bodies purified through mortification (the putting to death) of the flesh, became inextricably entangled in the European imagination.

Eventually, the Western world began to expand, taking its morality play about fatness and thinness along for the ride. As Europeans began to expand their scope, new people, new places, new languages, new cultures came into view. But the window in which white Christian Europeans so much as considered coexistence with their newfound global neighbors was short. Imperialist muscle flexing required that non-European, non-white people around the world be thought of in ways that made it only reasonable, only rational, that they should be subject to Europe's colonizing, "civilizing" forces. Historians of these colonial encounters, beginning with figures like Jennifer Morgan and Annette Kolodny, have traced a distinctive shift in the ways that colonized people and places were seen. What began in exploration-era prelapsarian fantasias of beautiful strong welcoming bodies and equally lush, paradisiacal, effortlessly productive land swiftly turned, with imperialism, into equally intense images of primitive, inhuman, bestial bodies and harsh, antagonistic landscapes, all of which had to be forced to submit to the superior will of the white Europeans who had the Christian God on their side. European-authored travel journals of the seventeenth century, tracing various North American adventures, spoke of Native peoples as being just as intelligent, strong, and beautiful as Europeans. Africans too were often viewed, by seventeenth-century eyes, as skilled, noble, and comely as Europeans.

After a century or so of imperial imposition and the start of an international slave trade, it had become apparent that these non-European people were not simply going to fall in line with European priorities. Colonized peoples swiftly became, if not quite their colonizers' enemies, then certainly problems to be managed. It is no coincidence that Europeans swiftly learned to view non-Europeans as "primitive," "uncivilized," "immoral," "shiftless," "ignorant," "savage," "lazy," "greedy," and of course "ugly." Here in the United States, in particular, those stereotypes came to have a fateful role in our current cultural fear and loathing of fat. The process, as historian Sabrina Strings has beautifully illuminated in her 2019 book *Fearing the Black Body: The Racial Origins of Fat Phobia*, was intimately connected with the enslavement of Black Africans. As such, the loathing of fatness has a great deal to do not just with imperialism and racism but also with classism, capitalism, sexism, and all their attendant dynamics of power and control.

As Africans were increasingly stolen from their native land and taken elsewhere to be enslaved, enslavers distanced themselves from those they held captive in multiple ways. Dehumanization is well known to scholars of slavery, genocide, and warfare as one of the ways to make the committing of atrocities more tolerable, even righteously justifiable. The more institutionalized slavery became in the United States, the more thickly the othering epithets of imperialism and white supremacy were applied. Black bodies, consequently, were increasingly viewed as primitive, animal-like, ugly, disproportionate, and inevitably lower and lesser than white bodies. This tendency lingers on: if you search your memory you might just be able to recall a recent Black US President, or a Black American woman tennis champion, whose detractors have frequently caricatured them as ugly, misproportioned, ignorant, illegitimate, and as "monkeys."

This, as Strings makes plain, is the work of the American eighteenth and early nineteenth centuries. The more common and visible slavery became, so too did the routine practice of dehumanizing Black people. Nor was it merely the bodies or appearances of Black people that were demonized. Damning moralistic claims were an inextricable part of these characterizations: Black people, enslaved or free, on North American soil or in Africa, were widely believed by whites to be inherently lazy beings that would rather steal than work, more interested in socializing, eating, drinking, fucking, and otherwise goofing off than anything else. In the words of Jean-Baptiste-Pierre Le Romain, friend to the French encyclopedist Denis Diderot and contributor to Diderot's 1765 *Encyclopaedia*, Senegalese slaves "are regarded as the most attractive in all of Africa . . . The coast of Angola, the kingdoms of Loango and the Congo produce an abundance of attractive *nègres* . . . Their penchant for pleasure makes them fairly unfit for hard labor, since they are generally lazy, cowardly, and very fond of gluttony." A hundred years later, racialized ideals of human beauty and value had firmly cemented the African not only as fat but as primitively, undesirably, and deviantly so. Strings cites an 1879 *Harper's Bazaar* essay entitled "The Fixed Facts of Beauty," which related of the "Circassian races" originating in the Caucasus that they ". . . take the Greek type as their model, with its slow and delicate curves, its perfect lines and slender elegance," noting that they "have certainly something in their eye very different from the African races who want bulging and bountiful flesh." "In this way," Strings writes, "this piece works to bolster the relationship between race and weight. Much like *Godey's Lady's Book* before it, *Harper's* promulgated the inferiority of African and Turkish races, said to delight in 'bulging' folds of flesh. And it simultaneously claimed the superiority of trim white people."

It is worth emphasizing that these ideas are the conceptual work of whites whose lives, success, and wealth were created by the Black people they enslaved and exploited. Slave labor was the engine of seemingly unbounded economic development in the eighteenth- and nineteenth-century United States and elsewhere, such as the sugar plantations of the Caribbean and South America. Without the Black bodies that were forced to perform it, the sheer amount of backbreaking labor required by the extraction economy that turned the land and its products into saleable commodities would have wealth accumulation slow at best for the New World's European and European-descended colonizers.

Although poor whites, including those who paid for their passage to the New World through selling their indentures, were always part of the labor landscape, they were few by comparison to the millions of black and brown-skinned humans whose muscle, sweat, intellect, and suffering cleared the land, built the plantations, planted and tended and harvested crops, kept the livestock, picked the cotton and the seeds from the cotton, and so much more. The economic, and eventually the cultural, success of the New World, and particularly North America, was the result of the theft, exploitation, and enslavement of African and African-descended Black people by European-descended white people.

Enslavement generated wealth, and wealth made many things possible for American whites: education, institution-building, patronizing the arts, philanthropy, social connections, fine living, social refinement—all the things that bespeak power, intellect, and goodness in our Christian-centric, capitalist, Eurocentric culture. Strings argues that during the eighteenth and early nineteenth centuries, white culture on both sides of the Atlantic came to develop an aesthetic of virtuousness that included all these things, especially the capacity for reason bred by a good education, and for a thoroughly Protestant godliness. Reason, judiciousness, and an appropriately Christian restraint when it came to all fleshly desires, they believed, could not but produce a thin, elongated figure whose lean lines advertised virtue.

This applied particularly to women, for whom public displays of virtue have always been more important. Lord Byron, so supposedly "mad, bad, and dangerous to know," was utterly taken by this retrograde and racist aesthetic. Famously, he struggled with his own tendency toward plumpness, believing that it led to stupidity and slowness, thus becoming one of the first white Europeans to be remembered for his deliberate weight-loss attempts. He did not limit his fear of fatness to himself, either, but saved special disdain for women who had the temerity to eat. In a well-known letter to his lover Catherine Lamb, written in September 1812, Byron wrote of his wife Annabella that "I only wish she did not swallow so much supper, chicken wings—sweetbreads—custards—& Port wine—a woman should never be seen eating of drinking, unless it be lobster sallad & Champagne, the only truly feminine & becoming viands." The only appropriate foods for women being legendarily light, prized, and expensive fit in perfectly with the politics of elite whiteness and, in particular, the thin, delicate, and valuable femininity to which elite white women in both Britain and the United States were encouraged to aspire.

Blackness remained ignominious, impoverished, disparaged in all the usual ways, particularly with regard to appearances and humanity. The Black body was automatically a disfigured body, a not-quite-human body, be it ever so fit and productive. Many enslaved women bore their enslavers' children, who were then enslaved in turn regardless of their racially mixed ancestry or even the lightness of their skin. American slavery's deliberately constructed legalities connected slavery to the condition of the mother. The white master's child could thus be born Black and enslaved and thus "lazy," "greedy," "ugly," "misshapen," "grotesque," "stupid," and frequently, as shorthand or as literal description, "fat."

Fat-hating is, in other words, not new. It is old and deeply ingrained, difficult to abandon even after we have considered its thoroughly rotten sources. It is also not necessarily about fat, as such. It is also about race, about class, about sex, and about power. This becomes manifestly clear after Emancipation, when, as many historians including Barbara J. Fields and Karen Fields have chronicled in their brilliant 2014 book *Racecraft: The Soul of Inequality in American Life*, expressions of outright racism became more pronounced because the system of subjugation provided by enslavement was no longer available. This is the era of the rise of the Ku Klux Klan as well as the romanticized "moonlight and magnolias" vision of Antebellum life. The early twentieth century, following in the wake of Reconstruction, brought with it the caricature of the eminently loyal, but dependent, ignorant, and fat Mammy, a character first developed in Harriet Beecher Stowe's pre-Emancipation *Uncle Tom's Cabin* (1852). After Emancipation she appeared, influentially, in Thomas Dixon's deeply white supremacist novel *The Clansman* and soon thereafter brought to life in film director D. W. Griffith's infamous *Birth of a Nation* (1915). The Mammy's round face, chubby neck, ample bosom, and voluminous but asexual body signified her uneducated but complacent devotion to whites and her own lowly, subservient lot. Fat and loyal, the Mammy became the Good Negro of the imaginations of those who wanted to romanticize and defend slavery. Her apotheosis arrived in the form of pancakes. Aunt Jemima, whose kerchiefed, beaming, fat-cheeked brown face has adorned self-rising flour products since the product line was founded in Missouri in 1889, has ensured that well over a century and a quarter of American breakfasters have literally been nourished on the image of a fat black woman's grinning servitude.

The Aunt Jemima image might not appear to rely on hatred or even racism to the casual observer. But it deliberately utilized the dynamics and the living memory of Black enslavement to reassure the (presumably white) buyer that their interests were being well served and their whiteness flattered by this happy-to-serve fat Black visage. Aunt Jemima represented a comforting acceptance of servitude, plus the certainty that she presented no challenge to white dominance. This message was deeply reassuring during what was an era not just of the end of slavery and the halting, difficult, always partial assimilation of Black people in the United States, but also an age of massive immigration. From the 1860s until well into the 1930s, it was immensely important for the purposes of the white, US-born, and "American"-identifying that there be a symbolic vocabulary that differentiated between those who belonged and those who did not, the deserving and the undeserving, the lives to which "native-born" white Americans might aspire and lives they would abhor and reject. In thousands of political cartoons imagery of fatness, filth, greed, poverty, and ignorance accompanied visions not just of Blacks but of dozens of groups of immigrants—Italians, Jews, Poles, Hungarians, even Swedes—not yet considered "white."

Over time, fat-hating has become so normalized and its priorities spread so broadly that its racist roots are rarely noticed. Yet it still holds enormous power, the power to dehumanize on the basis of a person's embodiment: the kind of body that exists in this kind of way is not fully human, not deserving of the things proper humans deserve. In contemporary America, calling someone "fat" therefore is never not an insult. "Fat" is humiliation and denigration, a way to instantly evoke disgust, revulsion, and shame. These reflexive, overwhelming associations and their attendant emotions foreclose our ability to think. Our analytical, rational brains cannot operate when we are writhing in shame, fear, and humiliation. Because we have made fat our foe for so many centuries, and because we have done it in the ways we have, fat has become something that dances us around by puppet strings. Because we have made fat so instantly, so intensely synonymous with shame and pain and the loss of humanity, fat has also acquired the power to deny us our rationality.

Eventually, as the title of Noel Ignatiev's germinal book *How the Irish Became White* suggests, assimilation did its work. With a wider sensibility of who might belong in a place like America, the overt racialization of fat became less widespread and overt. It did not vanish, of course. University of Colorado legal scholar Paul Campos has recently written about the aggressive use of fatness as a way of expressing prejudice against South American immigrants in Southern California, for instance. But as it turned out, there was a much more effective means of perpetuating and communicating this long-simmered abhorrence of fat and fat bodies. Medical science was rising in cultural importance, sophistication, and authority; furthermore, it allowed fat loathing to spread. Everybody, after all, has a body, and thus anyone might find themselves beset by the hateful, symbolically toxic and degrading affliction of fat.

In the United States, this began to take place during the same tumultuous and intense time period as Emancipation and the first massive waves of immigration, the second half of the nineteenth century. The Popular Health Movement, which had its roots in Jackson-era anti-intellectualism, spawned hundreds of books, lectures, and businesses that all revolved around the notion that lay people were perfectly capable of managing their own health. Popular Health thinkers, including the Reverend Sylvester Graham—who would be shocked to discover the sugary, kiddie-food fate to which his whole-wheat health crackers have been consigned—were highly skeptical of trained physicians. They might well have been, given that most of the scientific advances that shaped modern medical success were still to come. The upshot of this medical mistrust was the development of a deep and fateful American conviction that the individual was often his or her own best doctor.

This approach to health had a substantial moral component. Centuries of believing that moral virtue could be visible in the body manifested itself, to Popular Health believers, in the conviction that poor dietary and personal hygiene would result in moral and physical corruption, sickness, and perhaps even death.

The health of the bowels, particularly, was thought to be the key to a good, moral life and a healthy, robust body. Wholesome diet, which specifically included acres of unseasoned vegetables, unrefined grains, milk, and plenty of pure cold water, was the weapon with which red-blooded, virtuous Americans were to combat the insidious effects of luxury, decadence, and un-Americanness. Alcohol, tobacco, and often even meat were considered particularly intoxicating and harmful, but any overindulgence was seen as both sickening and sinful.

It was here that the health food movement and the American tendency toward dieting arguably have their most direct roots. An overindulged body was an ill body, an oversexed body, a body that craved constant and dangerous stimulus, a body in the process of self-destruction. Fatefully, this was a state of affairs that could often be detected by the naked eye: one would become sallow, slow, and fat. To be lean, quick, and clear complexioned was evidence of health and virtue.

Little wonder that as nineteenth-century Americans began, on the basis of European antecedents, to flock to their own natural springs and develop their own sanatoriums, they were relentlessly dieted, exercised, and treated to achieve a more optimum, health-preserving amount of fleshiness. These medical and medico-moral institutions, with their legions of attendants and nurses, doctors and orderlies, represent the first concerted medical effort to cure the problem of fat in America. From Battle Creek, Michigan to Hot Springs, Arkansas, Americans who could afford it visited these facilities to be treated for what ailed them, hoping to return home detoxified, energized, and bettered in soul and body.

As successive generations of medical innovation and invention arrived, they were likewise pressed into service against the menacing, multiplying flesh. As the discovery (and later, synthesis) of hormones knocked the biomedical world on its ear in the early years of the twentieth century, fantasies of regulating human physiology blossomed anew. The notion that exogenous hormones could rescue the run-down, the old, the impotent, and the tubby was seductive. Suddenly "glandular problems" seemed to be part of every diagnosis, and those who could afford to buy the "glandular extracts" that promised to solve them did so with enthusiasm. The fact that hormone tablets and elixirs and even injections did not actually do what was hoped for was largely ignored, at least for a while. Hope springs eternal, particularly where it involves being able to rescue yourself from a body that both signals and increasingly generates downward social mobility.

Before long, however, the new discipline of psychiatry seemed to offer a promising new avenue for eradicating the plague of fat. The work of Sigmund Freud and his many followers pointed to the family drama and neurosis to explain fatness. Mothers were to blame, they taught, for feeding their children in the wrong way in relation to the child's emotional and developmental needs during what Freud conceived of as the "oral stage" (roughly the first eighteen months of life) of psychosexual development. This is where we get the idea that an "oral fixation" leads to fatness, to say nothing of an enhanced tendency to blame mothers for anything and everything that might go wrong with their children. Later, other psychologists and psychiatrists would develop other theories about fatness: the idea that fat is psychic armor; the belief that fatness is a way of hiding from or delaying dealing with sexuality; the notion that fatness is the result of eating "aggressively" rather than displaying aggression in ways that could lead to interpersonal conflict; and so on. Some of these theories may sometimes be applicable in individual cases, but none of them can explain fatness as a human phenomenon across the board.

In the 1950s and 1960s, spurred by developments in research that emerged from the period of the Second World War, nutritional science became the new front line in the war on fat. Ancel Keys's work on starvation was only part of the picture. As research on vitamins and other nutrients escaped the realm of academia and policy, and research-driven awareness that nutrition could have a world-changing effect on health became a part of middle-class supper conversations, Americans turned to dietetics and nutrition science to provide new armament in the war against fat.

During my 1970s childhood, my mother combed the newspapers and health magazines for new reports from bioscience's command central that would help her slim down her disappointing, chubby daughter. When scientists declared that a low-fat diet would save us all from heart disease as well as getting rid of fatness, we ate low fat, at least for a while. The Atkins and Scarsdale diets came next, one of the precursors of contemporary high-protein, high-fat diets, which had me eating only about 700 calories a day as a tween and young teenager. For several years afterward I could not bear the smell or taste of an egg. Legions of weight-loss and "health food" cookbooks—which continue to this day to sell a version of the Popular Medicine shibboleth that virtuous food generates a virtuous, thin body—appeared in my mother's kitchen, with the result that bran muffins from the recipe originally published in the 1985 *Jane Brody's Good Food Book* remain a comfort-food favorite for me so long as applesauce is substituted for the half cup of oil called for in the recipe, just the way my fat-fearing mother used to make. At some point in the second half of the 1980s my mother stumbled into the world of "scientifically engineered" meal replacement "shakes" and declared the gritty, chalky, add-water-and-mix slurries my new weapon in the war against fat. They were horrible and gave me stomach aches, but I diligently drank them lest I be punished for going AWOL.

As human ingenuity opens new biomedical doors, we rush through them in the hopes of the ultimate weapon against fat. We have gone after fat with drugs—I am part of the last generation of fat kids whose parents and physicians gave them amphetamines to "boost the metabolism," which did little but render me a jittery, anxious fat kid. I later graduated to Dexatrim, an over-the-counter weight-loss pill that at the time contained the notoriously risky stimulant ephedra as well as phenylpropanolamine, a decongestant whose side effects include both appetite suppression and a heightened risk of stroke. But it could have been worse. Some weight-loss drugs, like the notorious Fen-Phen (fenfluramine/phentermine), have killed some of those who've used them hoping for victory against fat. Sometimes death has also come to those who've remodeled their GI tracts with surgery in order to force their bodies to use stored fat, though chronic malabsorption of nutrients is a more likely outcome. We've lined up for the chance to pay money to serve as de facto lab rats for ingenious food substitutes, like fats that our bodies cannot absorb and sweet-tasting things that provide no energy, only to discover that they may cause cancer (as in the case of saccharin) or uncontrollable leaking of greasy feces (the fat substitute Olestra). As we've become able, we've even begun to investigate our own DNA, hoping that perhaps finally there, in the twisted strands of our origins, we will figure out how to conquer the enemy that threatens to bring us down, if not with heart attack or high blood pressure then with what our culture insists is unlovable, lowering, horribly déclassé misshapenness.

Naturally, when biomedicine met demography in the early twentieth century, fat was part of the synergy. Infamously, it was the Metropolitan Life Insurance company that began, in the 1910s, to use height and weight as part of their demographic analysis to predict risk of death and thus allow them to maximize profits. Demographers and public health officials quickly banded together, slide rules and adding machines in hand, to work out mathematically the dangers of fat, literally calculating the perils of having a body that did not fit the norms. In an era in which previous centuries' leading causes of death— infections, epidemics, childbirth, accidents—were rapidly becoming problems that public sanitation prevented or that medicine could successfully treat, other causes of death such as heart attacks and cancer rose to the tops of the charts, where demographers promptly linked them, with or without actual evidence, to fat. No less an authority than Ancel Keys would later admit that the evidence did not, strictly speaking, provide particularly good support for this link, but he felt it was still reasonable simply because he found fat so unpleasant and disgusting. Thus fat officially became not just a personal problem or a source of disgrace, but a public health concern. But unlike cholera, which could be stopped with proper sanitation and sewers, or smallpox, which could be prevented by vaccine, only individuals could fight their bodies' tendency to accumulate fat.

The burgeoning economy and capitalist creativity of the post–Second World War years created the next field of battle in the war on fat: the weight-loss industry. The emphasis on fatness as an individual problem with an individual antidote, bolstered by an increasing interest in "health foods," created a market for weight-loss books and advisers. These "experts," many of whom had no relevant credentials, often did quite well for themselves by convincing people to pay for their insights on how to achieve a physically superior, aesthetically compelling body, one with the potential for admiration, desirability, and upward mobility. One of the most famous of these so-called weight-loss gurus was a self-identified "fat housewife" from Queens named Jean Nidetch who stumbled into creating a weight-loss support group among some of her fat-fearing 1960s neighbors. It proved enormously popular, popular enough that in 1963 Nidetch parlayed it into the familiar company Weight Watchers International (now known simply as "WW"). Weight Watchers soon became a publicly traded company on the New York Stock Exchange. Nidetch, already a weight-loss multimillionaire, ultimately sold the concern to the W. J. Heinz company in 1978 for $78 million; Heinz in turn sold it in 1999 to a private equity firm for $735 million. Today, despite the vast competition that has arisen in the fifty-seven years since its founding, WW International still makes vast sums of money. The 2018 annual report listed WW's revenue at $1.514 billion.

This dramatic rise in profit tracks perfectly with the expansion of the cultural role and intensity of the war against fat since the 1960s. The US weight-loss industry, which is to say the industry that makes money off the war against fat, is currently worth a record $72 billion annually according to *Business Wire*. It makes sense: capitalism loves a nice hungry war, and neoliberalism adores a problem that can be dropped with a stern finger waggle into the lap of the individual, the better to ensure that government remain untaxed by addressing whatever systemic causes may contribute to the mess and the individual can be made, metaphorically as well as literally, to pay for it. The war against fat is the best of both worlds. Follow the conflict, the fear, the need, the money.

Why, indeed, would we not rush to buy whatever armaments might help us win even a tiny battle against this slippery, disgusting, destructive foe? Fat stigma is everywhere, and lest you think my claim of fat people's dehumanization is a bridge too far, a 2019 report published in the medical journal *Obesity* bears me out. In this report, a comparison of results across four studies and about 1,500 respondents showed that "people with obesity" were blatantly dehumanized, believed to be "less evolved and less human" than their thinner counterparts. Other studies have confirmed this in a variety of specific environments, such as medicine and education. Fat-hating socialization starts very early. Researchers have found that even toddlers absorb the anti-fat attitudes of those around them, particularly their primary caretakers: although infants are perfectly happy to look at images of fat people regardless of how their parents may feel about fatness, toddlers whose mothers showed strong anti-fat bias were not. For these children—and in all likelihood most American children—to learn to communicate, understand, and absorb the messages sent by parents was to learn to hate fat. Let me be clear: we live in a culture in which even toddlers learn that fat people are unworthy of being acknowledged as human beings who we can look at with recognition and welcome.

What would you not do, what would you not give, what would you not pay if it offered you even temporary acknowledgement as a human being? What would you not do simply to be allowed to remain one?

Fat may well be our genuine enemy. This may be true in all the realms so far asserted and in realms we have yet to imagine. It is quite possible that as I sit here writing, my fat has already bought me a one-way ticket to an early, avoidable death. I suppose we'll all find out eventually. And yet. And still. I reserve the right to question the validity of any enemy, and the nature of any foe, presented to me in such totalizing and emotionally devastating terms that it compromises not only my personal ability to think, to evaluate, to discern, but also that of my culture. Coercion and manipulation, after all, are our enemies too.

4 FETISH

One day not so long ago the tiny Mennonite-run grocery store in the next small town over, on which I rely for Amish cheese and bulk baking supplies, suddenly sprouted a set of end cap shelves devoted exclusively to jars of coconut oil. Coconut oil is, shall we say, not exactly a traditional Mennonite ingredient. Yet there it was, jar after jar of the stuff, a testament to the depth and reach of a particularly strong and fashionable fat fetish.

Touted by health food enthusiasts as being almost as good for you, point for point, as actually being fat is claimed to be bad for you, coconut oil fans claim that it can reduce belly fat, reduce harmful LDL cholesterol, strengthen the immune system, prevent heart disease, curb appetite, and prevent Alzheimer's disease, to say nothing of keeping your teeth and gums gleaming and cavity free. Coconut oil has long been popular with vegans because as a fat that is 80 to 90 percent saturated, it behaves a lot like butter, which makes it especially useful for baking. But its current trendiness has nothing to do with the fact that you can make a pretty good puff pastry with it. Rather, a few currently trendy weight-loss diet regimens, like the ketogenic and "Paleo" diets, tout coconut oil as a wonder worker, and so it has become ubiquitous, even on the shelves of a little store in a small town in Ohio staffed by freshly scrubbed women in high-necked cotton dresses, sturdy shoes, and pleated white caps.

Mind you, according to the Harvard School of Public Health, the few daily tablespoons of coconut oil that anyone is actually likely to consume isn't enough to make much difference one way or another. But the actual functionality of an object has never been the point of a fetish. A fetish, in the broader, nonsexual meaning of the word, is an object that is worshipped for its associations, its symbolic content, its magical powers. In the United States, for instance, some people fetishize the Confederate flag as a touchstone for the rebellious, the anti-government, the independent, the southern, and, in addition, the racist and the white supremacist. In a very different direction, others fetishize old-school vinyl audio recordings as talismans of a time when they believe the music industry, or perhaps music itself, was somehow "truer" and "more real" than it is today.

And so it is with fat. In 2018, the Californian food writer and chef Samin Nosrat appeared in a Netflix television series based on her excellent 2017 cookbook, *Salt, Fat, Acid, Heat*. Each of the four episodes focused on one of the titular elements of good cooking. The very first to air? *Fat*. One can easily see why the producers would choose to kick off the series with this paean to everything unctuous. The episode is a bucolic, golden, luxurious affair set in Italy, where Nosrat leads the viewer through a playful yet worshipful investigation of olive oil, the fats in cheese and pork, and an utterly irresistible focaccia-making session. (The technique for focaccia shown in the episode, incidentally, is a sensual revelation to knead and shape and produces an exceptionally satisfying loaf.)

In this remarkable hour of television, the viewer is shown not only what to fetishize about this fat, but how and why. Fat's primal connection to the abundance of the land, the fact that it delivers flavor like nothing else, its luxurious looks and textures, and its connection to Italy's long-lived culture are all reasons to ooh and ah, to touch and taste, to pause reverently when tasting and close one's eyes for a moment in sensual reverie. Not a word is spoken about fat as a problem, an enemy, or as a problematic excess. Indeed, a largesse of fat is, in this particular bit of television, unequivocally a vehicle for wonder and shared joy. Moreover, it is a stamp of exclusivity and sophistication, and by association, the wealth necessary to travel. By the very fact of its demonstrations, Nosrat's *Fat* shows us that to understand fat in this way, to know how to luxuriate in it and to have access to the right kinds of fat in which to revel, is something that not everybody has.

Edible fat is not, of course, the same thing as human body fat. I would not want to suggest a false equivalency. One is taken into the body, the other is created by the body. Body fat may or may not have any relationship to culinary fat. That is to say: the fats we eat contribute energy to our bodies, but so do many other things. It's possible that some of the energy derived from fats we eat is eventually transformed, through the silent industry of the metabolism, into fat our bodies store. It's impossible to tell, though, and there's no magic or "like causes like" relationship: eating fat does not, in and of itself, cause the body to generate fat.

Edible fat and body fat are different things. Sensually speaking, they both offer distinctive and often deeply pleasurable experiences. They are symbolic in multiple ways good and bad. But we have strong feelings about both. We regularly make aesthetic judgments and decisions about them. Shall we blot the pizza grease off our slice or revel in its pepperoni-flavored unctuousness? Will we permit our jiggly thighs to do their thing in comfort, or are we going to Spandex those hams into trampoline-firm submission lest their jiggle be noticed? It depends, of course. What are we in the mood for? What makes us feel good, versus what makes us feel ashamed or guilty? Just how much pleasure are we willing to take in fat, and how much of that are we willing to have witnessed and known?

This is just as true when it comes to fat and sex. Fat, of course, is not everyone's sexual cup of tea. Given that humans are the complicated creatures they are, though, this is not saying much, since neither is anything else. Not all gentlemen prefer blondes, not all blondes prefer gentlemen, et very much cetera. But many people, whether they think of it in these terms or not, appreciate the sexual pleasures of fat: hips, butts, breasts, even the plumpness of kissable lips are very much dependent on fat.

Physical femininity and fat are, in a very real way, inextricable. There's an old, eye roll—inducing joke that runs "How do you make ten pounds of fat irresistible?" "Stick a nipple on it!" Not for nothing is "big naturals," meaning big breasts whose size is not thanks to surgery, a popular pornography category. Although breasts aren't the only place the body can deposit fat—and not everyone who has breasts and is fat has big breasts—it is also true that the glands and ducts that allow for milk production are roughly the same size in all bodies, which means that the amount of fat deposited in the breast is what determines its size. As with fat deposits anywhere else in the body, no one can choose how much the body will deposit where. The body's tendency to preferentially put fat into the breasts is doubtless vexing to people who'd rather not have big breasts or perhaps breasts at all, but it's a joy and a pleasure to those who find big, plump, weighty, jiggly breasts completely entrancing.

The same is true of hips and butts. The so-called "hourglass" or "Coke bottle" figure so often touted as the perfect womanly shape in our culture is due in part to fat. People with uteruses find that at puberty their hips tend to broaden. This is not just a matter of skeletal growth, it's a matter of sex-linked fat deposition. When puberty arrives, people assigned female at birth add fat at nearly twice the rate of people assigned male at birth. They add it in particular places, too: breasts, butt, hips, and thighs. Scientists believe this confers some advantages during pregnancy, childbirth, and lactation. More to the point for our discussion here, this fat pattern attracts a lot of attention both aesthetically and sexually, and according to the historical and artistic record this is nothing new.

But does this attraction and this attention that we pay to fatty feminine curves constitute a fetish? It depends on how you look at it.

In psychiatric diagnostic terms, a fetish is an inanimate object or a body part on which a person is sexually fixated and from which that person derives the lion's share of their sexual satisfaction. Some formulations of the definition hold that to be a fetish, the fetish object must be present if the fetishizer is to be able to reach orgasm. Certainly there are people who feel this way about fat bodies, and about specific parts of fat bodies including pendulous bellies, cellulite, back fat, and more. These people and their fetishes are, to paraphrase Douglas Adams, mostly harmless, much like the vast majority of other people's sexual quirks and foibles. After all, there are people whose sexuality is similarly concentrated on other body parts and states: some fetishists love armpits or hair, feet or fingernails, the skinny or the aged or the amputee. Why not fat?

Yet as I discovered when I wrote the first book on fat and sexuality back in 2000, a sexual fetish for fat is a bridge too far for many people. Many people, on hearing about the book, had a hard time even with the notion that that anyone could find fat bodies attractive at all. Initially I was baffled by this, then I was just confused. Relatively few people actually have fetishes that fit the classical definition, regardless of whether the fetish object is fat or feet or firearms (a very American fetish object indeed). But many people enjoy them and, furthermore, think nothing of defending their enjoyment. Why else would ample breasts and curvy hips, or stiletto heels and stockings, or for that matter the National Rifle Association, be so popular?

In the twenty years since I wrote that book, it has been my repeated observation that to put a name to a sexual attraction to fat is to invite being called a fetishist. The idea of having a "fetish," after all, seems suspicious to many people, abnormal, probably sick. Given the depth and intensity of our training to abhor and abjure fat, it also seems suspicious and abnormal and probably sick if one fails to hate it, let alone likes it in some way. This, to my way of thinking, is proof of our real fat fetish. We have created a fetish object of wrongness, of ugliness, of undesirability out of something common and generally benign. This is fetish as sympathetic magic: the thing becomes what we believe it to be, and it taints by association. Little wonder that the boundary between fat and thin is so unclear, so prone to shift, and so electrically charged. Every time we compartmentalize fat, accepting some as good and rejecting the rest as vile, tolerating this sort but violently rejecting that one, we transform it into a thing that has far more power than one would think something so profoundly associated with laziness and immobility ever could. Fat is a continuum. This is not a difficult thing to grasp. Fat comes in many varieties and manifestations. But all of them are fat. Only the magic we do through our thinking separates it into the tolerable and intolerable, the delicious and the poisonous. This is why we don't like to admit that there is even a family resemblance between the fat that cures what ails you, demonstrates your gourmet savoir faire, or fills out your voluptuous body . . . and the fat that might make people think you're ugly, stupid, uncultured, and whose bad reputation clings like the reek of old fryer grease.

Consider the disconnect between the kinds of fat consumption and enjoyment shown in the "Fat" episode of *Salt, Acid, Fat, Heat* and the kinds of fat that the average American might actually consume on an average day. Porchetta and pesto, prosciutto and focaccia glistening with fresh green olive oil are an absolute cornucopia of delicious fat. So, indeed, are a burger and fries and a milkshake. But the latter is, even when rendered in a high-concept way, a lowbrow meal. The whole gimmick of the Kobe beef burger and duck-fat fries with truffle salt lies in the collision of lowbrow foods and high-end ingredients, the interplay of louche and luxe. In America's mainstream food culture fat is undeniably a pleasure, but it tends to appear as a guilty, crass, and thoughtless one associated with the greedy maws of the masses. Thus Nosrat's fatty travelogue had to go not just anywhere but to Italy, with all its centuries of associations with high art and fine living, to establish fat as unquestionably being a realm of cultured, thoughtful, well-savored delight.

Fat tastes good and feels good. This is part of why it troubles us. The deep, originally Christian conflict about pleasure we inherited from our ancestors very much includes fat. The denial of fatty and fleshy foods like meat and butter is the cornerstone of centuries of Catholic fast day cuisine. But denial always generates tension. Desire precluded is not desire erased. Even the most devout believer might begin to feel deprived or wake up one Lenten morning with a terrible and unshakable craving. One of the towers on the majestic cathedral at Rouen, France, was reportedly built with the proceeds from priests selling permissions, aptly called "indulgences," a sort of spiritual hall pass that allowed good Christians to eat butter when they weren't supposed to. Are we really so willingly naive about our own lives that we can't glimpse the connection between buying an indulgence to eat butter and cream and our vows, spoken aloud, to go to the gym and work off the French fries we just ate?

But perhaps we do indeed fail to make the connection. We have, after all, shifted our frame of reference when it comes to our bodies; often we speak of sickness in the places where our ancestors might have talked instead about sin. To knowingly risk one's health, or even to believe that one might be doing so, is as immoral to many of us as knowingly risking our immortal souls was to our ancestors. We are well trained in thinking this way, our doctors and our media lecturing us sternly about fat and cholesterol, heart attacks and diabetes. Capitalism being what it is, we are also encouraged to make purchases that will either symbolically or actually mitigate our sinful ways. Low-fat prepared foods have, apparently permanently, joined our foodscape. Likewise, we are encouraged to use cookware with non-stick surfaces not merely because they can be so much easier to clean, but because they allow cooking with minimal fat or none at all. Conscious of the fact that fat is a dense source of energy—that is to say, it "has" a lot of calories—we are taught to ask for our salad dressing on the side, buy snack chips that are baked rather than fried, acquire air fryers for our kitchens, and endure the chemically engineered goo of thickeners created to mimic the mouthfeel of fats without our having to actually eat any. Every so often we are offered a particular fat and told that it is a "good" fat, that is, a fat that does not engage in the "bad behavior" of other fats. This is why my Mennonite grocery store is selling indulgences in the form of coconut oil.

Yet a glance at television commercials routinely takes the viewer on a fat safari: stretchy cheese on pizza, sizzling fat on a closeup of a burger, rivers of butter flowing over mashed potatoes, and bacon on or in or with practically everything. Any sojourn down any of America's countless carelessly congealed boulevards of strip malls and big-box stores yields the opportunity to encounter this fatstravaganza in real life, to consume fat in massive, even heroic quantities without so much as having to leave the upholstered comfort of one's car. We are constantly, perpetually confronted with fat as a temptation, an inducement, a seduction.

I use the word on purpose. Seduction feels so good. It is more than merely promising, it is burgeoning. Where the fat we eat is concerned, we fall for it more often than many people want to admit. But there is a double standard: wanting fat in your mouth can be excused; wanting your mouth on someone's fat cannot. Picture a hypothetical person sitting in their hypothetical automobile shuddering with disgust at the idea of sex with a fat person while they thoughtlessly, hungrily dunk a French fry into their milkshake and eat it. It's not difficult to imagine.

What, then, can we make of all the prurient enthusiasm straight women my age appear newly emboldened to express for the soft-in-the-middle "Dad bod"? Why does leading US plus-size fashion retailer Lane Bryant now offer a full line of sexy lingerie in an array of large sizes? How do we make sense of the 2019 decision on the part of international formalwear merchant David's Bridal to discontinue its policy of charging fat brides higher prices for their wedding gowns? And precisely how are we supposed to think about all the women who fit the current Centers for Disease Control statistics for the "average American woman," namely about 170 pounds and a size 16 or 18 in clothing? Are the millions and millions of people who are happily and enthusiastically desiring and having sex with these—arguably fat—women doing something that is somehow not pretty darn average?

There is, of course, precedent. Very little in the annals of human sexuality is new. There have always been people who have lusted after fat bodies. But we tend to be fairly private and secretive about our sexual likes, particularly when our culture does not share them. We don't know, for the most part, whether most people who found fat partners sexually attractive thought of themselves as being somehow strange or different. But we do know that in recent history, since the 1960s at least, there have been sexual undergrounds—some more and some less visible or organized—in which fat bodies are prized, even worshipped. Certainly not everyone who ever felt an attraction to a fat body or a fat person became or becomes part of one of these groups. Despite our contemporary assumption that divergences in sexual identity lead to the formation of community, the Lesbian, Gay, Bisexual, Transgender, Queer, Intersex, Asexual+ (LGBTQIA+) community being Exhibit A, not everyone feels drawn to forge a social circle based around their sexuality.

But some fat-loving people have felt that draw, enough that we have communities and organizations, networks of friends and more, who self-identify their sexual affinity for fat as part of their identity. Big Beautiful Women, or BBWs as our admirers often style us, are the preferred sexual objects of straight men who call themselves Fat Admirers or FAs. "Chubby chaser," a term viewed with some distaste in the straight fat-loving world, is more cheerfully accepted in gay men's circles, where chubs and chasers, and sometimes also big hairy bears, have their own websites, phone apps, weekend retreats, parties, and more that put them in contact with one another. BHMs, the Big Handsome Man counterpart to the BBW, can apply themselves to the communities that best fit their tastes. Perhaps predictably given the tendency of queer women's communities to organize around politics more than erotic specificities, there is no queer women's equivalent to "chubby chaser" or the world of Growlr hookups. The fat acceptance movement, however, has long had a robust following among queer women, whether because of their feminist commitment to dismantling fat loathing, their desire for fat women, or some combination. For a brief, sweaty, delicious moment in the 1990s, queer fat women's community gave rise to *FaT GiRL: A Zine for Fat Dykes and the Women Who Want Them* and also *Size Queen,* audacious and joyful DIY attempts to produce not just sexual community but also specifically queer, fat porn for and by fat queer women and trans people.

(Full disclosure: I was an avid reader, and many of the creators and artists responsible are friends of mine to this day.)

I suppose one could argue that there are many people who don't identify themselves as being part of these groups and communities who really ought to. This would, at least, help make sense of all the desire for fat bodies that seems to be flying around. If we could simply contain it, categorize it, put it in a convenient box with a handy label on the lid, it would certainly clear up any confusion we might have over what and who is supposed to be sexy, desirable, and wanted, and who will have to be content with the perverts, the fetishists, and the just plain weird.

Convenient for some, yes, but disingenuous for all. The truth, as it has the inconvenient tendency to be, is significantly more complicated. What seems apparent from the evidence of human behavior is that human desires occupy a vast continuum, one that perpetually resists our attempts to limit it. We are explicitly and implicitly taught not to acknowledge many types of sexual desires that our culture deems unacceptable. Until quite recently, in the historical scheme of things, one famously dared not acknowledge "the love that dared not speak its name," that of one man for another. We also do not like to acknowledge that attraction is not always, perhaps not even typically, as static and fixed as we are often encouraged to believe, or that we might desire many different people and attributes over the course of our sexual lives.

In my life as a fat queer woman, I have been sexually active with a range of partners tall and short, thin and fat. Burly masculine people with a bit of a belly are my crush-objects of choice, but I also believe there are far too many delicious kinds of human beings on this planet to count. I have never been puzzled in the slightest about whether bodies of many degrees and kinds of fat could be sexy. I knew quite clearly that they could.

Yet for many years I, like many other fat women I know, thought it very confusing when others found my fat body sexually attractive. Compartmentalizing fat, believing that some of it is acceptable and the rest unconscionable, is not just a theoretical exercise, you see. Yes, I enjoyed other fat bodies. But I felt a disconnect between their bodies and mine, my arousal and other people's. My body, or so I was socialized to believe, was unacceptable, unlovable, unwantable, unfuckable. Like many fat people I've talked to, I spent a few youthful years suspicious that those who showed sexual interest in me were either taking pity on me or indulging in a suspicious, probably unhealthy, fetish. Even after I got over that particular hurdle, I still often felt like I had to compensate for being fat in some way or another, even when other people clearly desired me. For the record, this is not a helpful or healthy context in which to begin one's sexual life.

Then, in my early twenties, I had a horrible fortnight. I went on one date that ended with my date becoming inappropriately aggressive, grabbing handfuls of my body and squeezing them hard enough to leave bruises while continually growling "I just can't get enough of you!" and so on. I told them to back off, that they were hurting me. When my protests were ignored, I extricated myself through the time-honored expedients of a solid knee to the crotch and a stacked wooden heel stomp to the instep only to have my would-be date rapist snarl "You should be grateful anyone wants to fuck you, you fat whore!" at my back as I slammed my car door.

A week and a half later I went out on another date, only because I had promised a friend I would let her fix me up with someone she knew. To my surprise this resulted in my eating Turkish food that evening with an openly self-identifying fat fetishist. He was an older, well-off man, and he proposed a sort of sugar daddy situation where I would indulge his desires to gratify himself by rubbing his penis against and in between the folds of my fat body and he would . . . pay for things, I suppose. I never found out, because the idea of having my body objectified that way made me anxious and uncomfortable, so I turned him down. He seemed cheerful enough about the rejection, at least at first, but when he walked me to my car he asked me to reconsider. When I said no a second time, he told me I should be grateful that he asked, because fat girls like me "just don't get that many chances to have someone worship their bodies." I rode the subway home feeling weirdly that I had been scolded, and also worrying that maybe he was right.

I was soaking in the tub later that night when I realized what had gone on. By that point in my life it had become abundantly clear that people were interested in me and obvious that my fat body was not necessarily a drawback to finding sexual partners. To some of them, in fact, it was a major part of the attraction. At the same time, when I refused people sexual access to my fat body, they immediately insulted it. They did not insult *me*. They insulted my fat, doing their best to undermine and manipulate me with the stigma of the same fat they'd been begging for moments before.

This, I concluded, was some fucked-up doublethink bullshit. Yet it had taken an attempted date rape and a condescending sugar daddy wannabe for me to even notice it was happening. This was because I had been indoctrinated with the appropriate compartmentalization of fat since childhood and inoculated with the feelings my culture demanded that I learn how to feel about myself. I learned it from every "it's a shame you're so chubby, you've got such a pretty face" and every maternal sigh of "I suppose eventually someone will probably date you for your personality." I internalized it from ads, from television, from watching my mother on her seemingly eternal diet, from the stack of *Playboy* magazines in the bathroom in my divorced dad's rented duplex. Occasionally I was simply told, straight to my face, by someone who wanted to see me wince. In those moments, part of me knew that it was just gratuitous cruelty talking. But gratuitous cruelty only put into words the messages I had been receiving from everywhere else. It is not impossible for cruelty to wear the mask of accuracy.

After all, it had not escaped my notice that fat made women miserable—or rather, what women had been taught to believe about fat made them miserable, and not infrequently made them make themselves even more miserable as an attempt to escape from fat. Inadvertently I learned which bathroom in my high school was the one favored for after-lunch bouts of bulimic vomiting, and knew which of the most popular and pretty skinny girls made their way in and out of that bathroom amid the noise of near-continual toilet flushes that announced as much as they masked. A friend's mother, an elegant and willowy former fashion model, spent months hospitalized due to anorexia. My own mother, she of the Liz Tayloresque curves, snarled and raged against the same recidivist fifteen pounds she repeatedly lost and gained throughout my childhood and adolescence: there is not a single photo of her from that era where she does not look tense and pained, where she is not visibly holding in every abdominal muscle in the attempt, as she put it, to "look decent."

In my twenties I found myself the frequent confidante of other women's fat anguish. Women, and not a few gay men of my acquaintance, would come to me for commiseration when they worried that they would get dumped, or not dated at all, because they were fat. Or at least "fat," which is to say that they were afraid of being found undesirable and the shorthand "fat" was the only word they had with which to say so. Somehow it seemed safe to them to come to me, the undeniably fat person in their lives. Perhaps they wanted the comfort of comparison, to reassure themselves that at least they weren't as fat as me. Many seemed to take comfort in my telling them that they were wonderful and lovely and smart and who cared what they weighed or whether they had a bit of a belly or whether their thighs were thick? I learned to carry tissues in my handbag, and keep some on my desk, because when fat angst was in the weather report there was often a rain of tears to go with it. As long as I empathized with their worries and flattered their beauty, they seemed to feel safe revealing their deep anguish about fat.

Eventually, however, I stopped being the Fat Friend. Not because I stopped being fat or for that matter friendly, but rather because the kind of support I was willing to give started to change. My friends wanted the safety of empathy, but what I found myself dispensing were reality checks. Why was it, I asked them, that these men they were interested in got to be so damn picky? Who made that rule? What kind of blue-ribbon-winning paragons were these male people, that they were entitled to summarily reject a person because her butt was not the precise size, shape, density, and degree of jiggliness that they found to be optimal? I turned the problem of fat angst around and asked pointed questions about what was really at stake. Having had more than a few people express sexual interest in me but be unwilling to consider me girlfriend material in any public way, I'd come to realize that whether someone finds you fuckable and whether someone thinks you're sufficiently high-status to suit their self-image are two different things. My friends' desirability was never really what was in question. I knew that. But it proved surprisingly difficult to get my friends to believe me that the problem they were facing had far more to do with male entitlement than about their bodies or their fatness or lack thereof. This was annoying, but not surprising. Fat-hating and body-loathing are purpose-built to derail and deflect, to leave individuals believing the worst about themselves rather than being able to detect the ways their lives have been poisoned by ideologies of status and power.

Philosopher Kate Manne, in her award-winning 2018 monograph *Down Girl: The Logic of Misogyny*, declares that in essence, sexism is the theory and misogyny is the practice, the "long arm of the law" of sexism that punishes in the name of enforcement. This analysis, rather than getting bogged down in idiotic qualifiers about how individual misogynist actors might subjectively feel about women—a straw man if there ever was one—sheds light on what misogyny does. In so doing, Manne gives us a critical insight about women's participation in their own repression: even dogs readily learn how not to do things that result in their getting swatted on the nose.

Sexism declares that women are not people but rather things that men are owed: their energy, their attention, their bodies, their reproductive capacity, their labor, their affection are all things to which men are entitled. Sexism further insists that since women are things, they may be scrutinized at any time. Similarly, it asserts that women are obliged to be beautiful, appealing, desirable to men. Misogyny makes it clear what happens to women who do not comply. Those who do not follow the rules, or at the very least demonstrate that they are trying their hardest to follow the rules, pay the price. Rejection, isolation, exclusion, poverty, insults, assaults. It's all punishment for the offense of failing to do what women are supposed to do—namely, not be fat. What else to call the fact that research has proven that as women become fatter, they are paid less, while this is not true for men? How, otherwise, to interpret numerous international studies that show that fatter women suffer a higher incidence of domestic violence, and that the violence they face tends to be more dangerous, even lethal? What else can we call it when a fat woman who is raped is told, as so many fat women are, that she should count herself lucky that anyone wanted to fuck her at all?

We cannot be remotely surprised that a body that is feminine and desirable yet somehow devoid of fat has become a staple goal for women. It does not matter that the goal is unattainable. One just tries to survive, and, with luck, not come in for too much punishment. It is not an accident that women's ability to be and remain thin has become the insignia of our capability and value. No wonder at all that we become our own police force, our own torturers and jailers and sometimes our own murderers, or that women turn on themselves, one another, and even on their own children when it comes to fat. In a culture where men hold (and have historically held) the lion's share of power and wealth, the threat of men's disapproval is the threat of impending disaster. This is why women can berate and starve ourselves, ferociously abuse and mistreat other people including our children, and yet believe in the bottoms of our hearts that we are doing it "for their own good." It is why so many of us grow up believing that just maybe, if we manage to make ourselves absolutely perfect, we might be able to escape the fate of being unloved, excluded, discarded. It is why we suck up headlines about celebrities' weight changes and sit, riveted, in front of *The Biggest Loser* and *My 600 Pound Life*. This is how we learn, like the woman I mentioned in the opening of this book, to use the phrase "I feel so fat" in place of saying "I am afraid," "I'm feeling insecure," "I worry that I'm unattractive," or "I feel unworthy of love and it hurts."

Fat, as the title of the old Susie Orbach book succinctly put it, is a feminist issue. Making a fetish out of fat, in all the various ways that happens, is a patriarchy problem. Whether fetishized in food, in the bedroom, or as the essence of all that is unlovable and disastrous, the fetish has everything to do with power, with status, with racism and sexism and classism. Not for nothing was I warned, as my research shows so many other white fat women friends have been as well, that if we stayed fat, only Black or Arab men would find us attractive. "They like that sort of thing," my mother insisted, making it once again clear that a desire for fat was suspicious, foreign, abnormal.

I have come to believe that our well-trained disgust at the idea of a sexual fat fetish is just a distraction. Goggling at the freaks and weirdos, singling the fat and the fat-desiring out as spectacle and as a cautionary tale, keeps us from noticing our real, and very much shared, fat fetish. This fetish rests, as so many others do, in status and authority.

When fat connotes sophistication, good taste, wealth, and especially control, it becomes precious, an indulgence to envy to precisely the same degree that it is rare. Think of the perfect hourglass figure, the impressive Kardashian buttocks that are (a) a correct skin color for a racist society's enjoyment and (b) disciplined out of any unruly jiggling. Imagine the heirloom breed ham or olive oil from centuries-old trees painstakingly husbanded and harvested from one's family farm. The less attainable the fat, the more uncommon and specific its attributes, the more desirable it becomes.

Common, imperfect fat is disaster. When it is too easy to come by, when it shows up and sticks around whether we want it or not, when it seems to have a mind of its own and refuses to follow the wholly imaginary rules we want it to obey, it is hateful, shameful, an embarrassment. The Kobe beef burger and duck-fat frites made in a kitchen ruled by a celebrity chef is a little too obvious a gimmick, a little too easy to come by, to escape the taint. The fat woman, in particular, is also too obvious, and too obviously a bad woman, an undisciplined and selfish creature, to be accepted. Merely to fail to punish her is offensive. Desire? How could anyone desire a disaster?

And yet most of our bodies, at some point or another, make it clear that there is only so much that we can control. Self-discipline is all well and good, but bodies are only so amenable to force. To loathe one's self, to view one's body as a betrayal and a disaster, to struggle endlessly to hit a notional and moving target for one's appearance just because it is so publicly and noisily fetishized seems to me like preemptive self-punishment, as if others can't hurt us if we can hurt ourselves badly enough first. Alas. Like coconut oil, self-loathing is unlikely to do what we want to believe it will, and it doesn't even have the redeeming virtue of being a decent substitute for butter in a chocolate-chip cookie.

5 FIGURE

I am not sure how I kept myself from crying until after the door was closed.

It was 1999, and I was deep in the process of interviewing people as part of the research for my book *Big Big Love*. It was to be the first book on the market that dealt with fat people and sexuality. Because it was novel and I had no idea if there would ever be another book on the subject (I'm pleased to say that there have been—and that I wrote a second edition of my own book) it seemed imperative that I make it reflect as many experiences as I could manage. To that end I had put out calls for interviews, and in due course my home office loveseat cradled big butts of all persuasions and backgrounds and sizes, hour after hour, for weeks.

As all of us who have conducted sexuality research discover rather quickly, it much more resembles a semi-forgotten minefield than it does a stack of back issues of *Penthouse Forum*. One becomes as accustomed to hearing stories of appalling trauma as one does to hearing tales of joyous romps and multiple orgasms. I had been holding up okay, for the most part, maintaining that critical bit of emotional distance between myself and my informants. But then one afternoon an interviewee said something that shocked me, and the knowledge hurt so badly I felt almost heartbroken.

A butch dyke I had seen around town, one I'd always thought sexy but whom I'd never had occasion to get to know, had volunteered for an interview. Now they sat across from me detailing their plans to seek sex reassignment, up to and including the language they knew they had to use with a therapist in order to acquire "the letter" to take to a physician.

"It's not because I really want to be a man so much," they confided, leaning in, "I love being a dyke. But I just can't take being a fat woman in this world much longer. I can't say that to a therapist of course. They'd never write my letter. And I know that all I have to do is just get rid of these tits and things'll be better. I'll still be fat. That's fine. But I can't be a fat woman. I can't be a fat woman, not anymore."

I didn't mind the thought of another butch becoming a trans man. I knew a small but growing number of guys who'd taken that path and I'd never been anything less than happy for them when they got to do the things that made them feel so much better in their skin. But this was different. My interviewee's fat pain was clearly enormous and ran very deep. But my interviewee did not say they wanted to be thinner. They didn't really even seem to want to be a man. The desperate desire my interviewee expressed was specific and pointed: to cease to be a fat woman.

After the interview was over and we said our goodbyes, I sat on the couch still warm from my interviewee's body, sobbing my way through the nearby box of tissues. Was it so unbearable, truly, to be what I was, to live in a fat female body? Did my interviewee experience the same horror being around other fat women as they did recognizing that they were seen as one themselves? Would it really be so much better to be a fat man than a fat woman? And why was it breasts that made the difference?

Let me say for the record that I have no bad feelings for my interviewee. Whatever might have transpired for them, I hope and pray that they are out there somewhere delighted beyond measure by the body they occupy today. I owe them one: they made me think hard and long about the fat figure.

As I have now been arguing for several dozen pages, all fat is created, but not all fat is created equal. Fat is classed and raced, sexed and gendered. Whether or not we have visible excess fat in our bodies, along with how much there is of it, has deep

FIGURE   101

meanings for our culture—or at least we have made it have such meanings. This includes the shapes fat creates, the figures it produces. We cannot mold our own fat into the specific shapes we want or control where our bodies deposit it, yet our lives are molded by the forms that fat takes.

Biology decides whether we deposit fat and where. In general, babies and toddlers wear their fat everywhere, much to the delight of aunties like me who like smooching chubby little arms and legs and cheeks and pretending to nosh on fat little toes. You have to nibble baby fat while you can, because baby fat eventually ebbs, and one is left with a body that is, for lack of a better word, kid shaped. When the hormone storms of puberty begin to arrive, though, it all changes again. The bodies of most people assigned female at birth begin to selectively accumulate fat in the hips, buttocks, thighs, and breasts. The bodies of people assigned male at birth generally don't. Later in life, the bodies of people assigned male at birth are more likely to accumulate fat in the torso, particularly in the belly. This is the source of many of our unexamined expectations, and consequently also our unexamined responses.

I use the phrase "assigned male/female at birth" for a reason here. For any number of reasons, the visual diagnosis of sex that a doctor makes when they look at a newborn's genitalia may not be correct. There are many people whose sexual biology does not entirely conform, for an array of causes both spontaneous and intentional, to what biology expects "male" or "female" bodies to be. There are even more people whose gender does not line up with the cisgender expectations of our culture—that people assigned female at birth will be women and feminine, while people assigned male at birth will be masculine and male. And fat is in the middle of all of it.

We tend on the whole to interpret fat as feminine. The much-vaunted "hourglass" figure I've mentioned previously is the classic example of feminine fat, just the right amounts in just the right places to swell just the right body parts to just the right proportions. But equally as feminine in terms of our associations is cellulite, the places where the skin over a fat deposit is dimpled or bumpy thanks to the strength of the connective tissue binding the skin to its underpinnings despite the fat cells that occupy the spaces in between. As it happens, cellulite knows no sex or gender, although it's more common in people assigned female at birth thanks to those pubertal fat deposits. But people assigned male at birth can and do sport cellulite. Yet somehow, you will never see ads for cellulite reducing creams or wraps or "blasters" aimed at men. First of all, men are not tasked with the same exacting adherence to attractiveness

FIGURE 103

standards as women, which is part of what makes those expectations so sexist. But even if they were, we still might not see cellulite-fighting weaponry aimed at men simply because cellulite is considered a female form of fat.

We extrapolate social meaning from many aspects of the body. We grow up hearing repeatedly that tall men are born leaders, or at least natural basketball stars. Watch a few Disney movies or read a few fairy tales and you'll be well indoctrinated in the theory that evil, wicked, cruel people are all ugly, old, or both. Big breasts mean a woman is more feminine and sexually free, while small breasted women are uptight and unfeminine. Muscular, athletic men are more virile than dudes with potbellies. Or so we tend to believe. It's rare that we say these things out loud, or even articulate them to the point where we could say them aloud if we wished. These tacit beliefs in the meaning of the body are cultural shibboleths, truisms we all seem to know and understand, whether or not we are in agreement. We use them to make sense of the world.

In the big picture, this works pretty well much of the time. So long as bodies look roughly the way we expect them to, meaning that the physical characteristics we encounter are more or less as we expect them, we are content that we know where a particular human being fits in our received hierarchies of identity. So long as this is true, we are unlikely to pause or question our reflexive assessment of what and who a person is. As with so many things we use to make sense of the world, we observe bodies in passing without really thinking about them, our brains making the connections and associations seemingly on their own, without our conscious involvement.

This is, of course, one of the reasons we tend to be so shocked when bodies do not behave or look as we have been conditioned to expect. We go through life seeing mostly what we expect to see, our stream of understanding flowing along at the pace to which we are accustomed. When we encounter something unexpected, our brains have to hit the brakes, sometimes hard and fast, and we lurch erratically, victims of our own inertia.

Bodies simply don't always do what we think they should or look the way we assume they will. Biology is not bound by our selfish desire for convenient ways to know things about other people without having to pay too much attention or, heaven forfend, ask. Mother Nature is a lot more creative than we are. Sometimes people assigned female at birth, like me, have bodies that store their fat on a more male-patterned plan. In my case, it's due to a fairly common though not well understood biological condition called Polycystic Ovarian Syndrome (PCOS). As the name suggests,

FIGURE   105

the most characteristic sign is ovarian cysts; my own ovaries, which I've seen thanks to the generosity of the surgeon who performed my hysterectomy, had regular little rows of cysts that grew all along the outsides in what doctors consider the classic "string of pearls" presentation. The syndrome's external signs are a lot easier to see. One of the classics is the tendency to accumulate fat in the belly in the way we usually associate with men, rather than the expected fat hips, butt, and thighs we associate with people assigned female at birth.

I don't much mind that I'm shaped like this. To me it's just one of the ways a body can be. But the same is not true for everyone with PCOS. Some cisgender women with PCOS that I have known find their potbellies depressing and infuriating, feeling like their body fat is actively trying to undermine their femininity. But I also know other people who enjoy this aspect of PCOS bellies. I have known several people assigned female at birth but whose preferred gender expression is masculine of center who find having a big belly an asset in telegraphing masculinity to the world. A big belly is not a big belly is not a big belly, in other words. It may be a blessing or a burden, depending entirely on what sex or gender it is that you wish the world to perceive.

People assigned male at birth can experience something analogous, though it's hips and butts and thighs instead of bellies that are the issue. Stereotypically, male-identified people have shoulders that are the same width as their hips or wider, with broader shoulders being associated in the popular imagination with greater masculinity. But bodies exist in all kinds of shapes. Some people assigned male at birth accumulate thick thighs, wide hips, big butts, and sometimes breasts. They might have these instead of the big bellies we expect big dudes to have, or in addition to them. Whichever it is, there's a high likelihood that the man in question is going to see this fat, and these parts of his body, as a serious crisis. Often men presume that these body shapes are a sign of a medical crisis, though that's usually not the case. A tendency toward female-pattern fat accumulation might be a signal of lower than typical testosterone, but medically speaking this is only very rarely cause for panic. No, the crisis here is all about gender. Thick thighs and padded hips, in the lexicon of fat, equal "feminine." Male privilege might rule the world, but it can't withstand juicy hips and a fat ass.

What to do, what to do about this unruly fat, this substance that doesn't give a damn for your tired old gender norms and biological bell curves? Not much, as it turns out. Despite the many claims made for exercises that target particular "problem areas" and internet clickbait promising that you can do "one

FIGURE   107

stupid thing" to get rid of belly fat, that's simply not how fat works. Just as you can't intentionally cause your body to accumulate fat where you want it by, say, rubbing cheesecake on your abdomen, you can't get rid of it with sit-ups either. When the body metabolizes its own fat, it takes a little bit from all over. What appears to be site-specific fat loss— for instance, noticing that someone's face or ankles look thinner—is really the consequence of fat loss in areas that didn't have as much fat deposited in the first place. Where faces are concerned, we also notice change simply because we spend a lot of time looking at them. We are intimately familiar with faces in ways we aren't with, let's say, thighs, and so we notice small changes more readily.

The truth is that bodies put their fat where their genetic and hormonal marching orders tell them to. It has zero to do with anything we do or don't do, anything we want or don't want. Why, then, do we hang so much meaning and so many layers of significance on what bodies do for their own inscrutable reasons? When male-identifying people have curvy hips and thighs or big butts, people often assume they're gay. Some of my transmasculine friends—people assigned female at birth whose sex and/or gender are now somewhere on the masculine side of the spectrum—regularly curse the curvy, chunky butts or hips that they worry may out them as trans. On another side of the gender spectrum, several of my transfeminine friends have been scolded by their doctors, and on a few occasions have even been denied necessary medical treatment, because they gained weight and their bodies happened to deposit fat in their bellies. It may not appear particularly feminine to have a potbelly, but it isn't exactly as if you can effectively instruct your body to store fat in more gender-affirming locations instead of the places it actually does. Physicians know this full well, and yet these doctors felt that by having fat bellies, my trans women friends were not doing enough to demonstrate that they were genuinely committed to being women. "If you don't look enough like what I think a woman should look like, I will refuse to give you the care you need to be a woman," seemed basically to be the gist of it. I wonder, would those doctors say the same to cisgender me on the basis of my belly? Cisgender or trans, we have an equal amount of say in the matter of where our bodies put their fat, after all.

My dear friend, the wonderful trans writer and performer S. Bear Bergman, has often commented on the differences in how he's been treated since he's been a man. One of my favorites is his comment that now, when he orders a Coke at a restaurant, he actually gets one, not a Diet Coke with a slice of lemon floating accusatorily in it. It was thanks to this comment, and

FIGURE   109

others like it, that it finally dawned on me why I was so upset, back in the 1990s, by that charming masculine soul on my loveseat and their declaration of intent to make a gender transition. My anguish had everything to do with gender, but not really with changing it. What unmoored me was my interviewee's clear goal to abandon femaleness specifically in order to escape the prejudice they faced as a fat woman. It broke through my own equivocations and the layers of thick skin I'd acquired out of necessity as a fat woman in this culture and rubbed my face firmly in the reality of the gendered humiliation and abuse that fat women deal with every day.

When Yasmin Sokkar Harker, a member of the faculty at the Law School of the City University of New York, produced her widely cited annotated bibliography of the legal literature on fat discrimination in 2015, she found she needed to include a section on "Fat Discrimination as Sex Discrimination;" in its introduction, Sokkar Harker writes, "Fat women are considered unfeminine and bear additional stigmatization by family, employers, and health professionals." The intensity and magnitude of the situation is deceptively minimized by the legal formality of the sentence. That word, unfeminine, is a critical one. As has been noted previously at some length, to be a fat woman in our Western culture is to do "woman" incorrectly. The proof is in the misogyny, in the studies that have shown that fat women are more likely to be convicted in criminal proceedings than thin women, more likely to be underpaid than both thinner women and almost all men, and that they face significant hiring and promotion biases in the workplace. To be a fat man is not necessarily to do "man" incorrectly, but to be one whose fat exists in a pattern associated with femininity is definitely to do "man" the wrong way. The infamous exclusionary phrase on every gay men's personal ad since at least the late 1980s when I became aware of them in the back pages of urban arts-and-culture weekly papers is "no fats, no femmes." The two can exist independently of one another, but the fact that they are so consistently paired as being something many gay men find repellent is telling.

Fat appears to have an astonishing power to interfere with sex, with maleness and femaleness and our expectations thereof. To be fat, and especially to "wear" that fat in unexpected or uncommon ways, is to do sex and gender fundamentally wrong. It is not one's behavior, or one's feelings, or one's choices that are incorrect; one's sex and gender wrongness is literally under one's skin.

Some years ago, hanging out with some of the members of my fat girl posse talking about sex, a friend archly noted that "What these thin women who look at us so funny don't understand is that a lot of us have places of interest where thin women

FIGURE 111

don't even have places." The laughter resolved into a conversation about those places, the body parts some fat people have for which there are no actual names. We debated what name would suit the tender-skinned swells at the tops of some of our upper, inner thighs, and whether back fat needed different names depending on where on the back it was. We determined that the fat pad on the top of the arch of the foot was the Mary Jane, after the style of shoe with a strap across the arch. My husband's contribution was to christen the area on the downward curve of a fat behind, leading to the top of the thigh, as "the helipad." It was the place where one came in for a landing, he observed.

In the years since I have had variations on the same conversation with other friends, struggling to think up better, more evocative names for things like a hanging belly, which the medical profession likes to call an "apron." Frequently we've wondered aloud about the particularly pungent words we have for a fat pubis, neither of which are medical and both of which—"gunt" (a portmanteau of "gut" and "cunt") or "FUPA" (an anagram for "Fat Upper Pubic Area")—are intentionally sexist and demeaning. There's a similar streak of nastiness that gets applied to men with fat deposits on the pubis, something that in some cases makes the penis appear smaller, especially when it is soft. The stereotypes of the fat man with the little dick and the fat woman with the enormous pussy have everything to do with our expectations of what genitals are supposed to be. Men are supposed to have a presence, ideally a large and protruding one, between their legs, women are supposed to have an absence, nothing at all protruding from between their legs.

Fat bodies, like some (though not all) intersex, transgender, and transsexual bodies, may tear this set of expectations up from the roots. It is deeply disturbing to many when they do. Surely women can never be allowed to have a fleshy presence between their legs, especially not one that is visible when they are clothed, and under no circumstances is it to be larger than the average penis. Surely men must always have groins that are as chiseled and sleek as a GI Joe doll's, save for the mighty penis and scrotum whose size and hardness tell us everything we need to know. To do otherwise is to have done wrong, and to have done wrong is to deserve punishment. The subsequent mocking, ridicule, cruel "jokes," and mean-spirited internet memes work by insisting that these bodies are wrong, that these people cannot even manage to wear their genitals correctly. All the wrongness that is projected onto fat bodies is projected onto the fat crotch in a concentrated form. As centuries of homophobia and transphobia have taught us, to declare a person's sexual organs and sexual activity to

FIGURE   113

be wrongly constituted and wrongly existing, is a way of excluding that person and people like them from full humanity.

This is why I find it so noteworthy, when I look back on that interview twenty years ago, that my interviewee was not seeking to become less fat. To my interviewee, fat was not the problem: I remember fondly their beer-bellied swagger and the wink and smile with which, at one point in the interview, they patted their belly and said they appreciated having some weight to put behind their thrusts during sex. Their problem was not their queerness, not their sexual opportunities, and not their fat. Their problem was that there was not a world in which they could live as a woman in the fat body they had and not be reminded constantly that they were doing it wrong. Certainly, as a masculine-of-center woman, they were likely to be reminded of that anyhow; butch women, may God bless them every one, are well aware that they are doing "woman" wrong in the culture's eyes by discarding conventional femininity. But when my interviewee found themselves stuck in the crosshairs of a queer-hating, transphobic, fat-hating, woman-hating society, the easiest thing to try to change, or perhaps the easiest thing to reconcile themselves to losing, was not the fat but the figure, the breasts that marked them out as something at which they were a failure as long as they were fat.

The fat figure, I believe, can teach us a lot. Fat is hated most where it conforms least. The patriarchy requires a hierarchy of bodies and power in order to function. This hierarchy requires bodies that are dependably formed, shaped, and proportioned, in order that one might know at a glance where a particular body belongs on the ladder of status, power, and authority. But Nature, in Her infinite wisdom, produces a rich, wild diversity of human bodies. Bodies are not answerable to our egos or our desires or even our cultural expectations, only to the instructions of DNA and biochemistry and environment and epigenetics, that mysterious translation of shared experience into biological tendency. In so doing they whisper some difficult truths about what exists without and beyond these power structures on which so many of us depend for our own status and power. In its spontaneity and catholicity, appearing where and when it does and not when and where we want it to, fat defies our belief that we somehow deserve what power we have because we are intrinsically somehow made of better, purer, more tractable stuff. That sex, gender, race, and class are deeply entwined in our compartmentalization of human fat is not a coincidence. These are the rubrics through which

FIGURE   115

we rationalize power and exert control—or try to, at any rate, including over an object, a substance that routinely, seemingly willfully, defies our attempts at mastery. Fat doesn't give a sweet and fancy goddamn what we want. For the most part we abide it only because we have no choice.

We might ask, then, what we believe fat is, given that our bodies must contain it or die. How do we understand something so ubiquitous yet intransigent, so resistant to our will? Is it simply a metaphor for humanity, in that we all contain the seeds of our own demise if not our own undoing? Or is there something more sinister that occupies the bunting of our double chins and love handles?

Perhaps the answer is that fat is sublime, in the original nineteenth-century Romantic philosophical sense of the word. The sublime, in this context, is an experience of the natural world as being something larger than one's self, something one cannot control, a thing that is simultaneously marvelous and dangerous and whose superhuman nature simultaneously humbles and exalts. Fat is within us, yet also beyond us. It is spontaneous and wild, and we fear its uncontrollability. It absorbs our attempts to bend it to our will without the slightest hint of struggle, and we can rant and rail at it just as we might at the ocean or the entire universe and produce only what Shakespeare might call "sound and fury, signifying nothing." That is the moment of sublimity: the awe as well as the terror of facing nature in all its independence from our humanity.

Let us say, then, that this object, fat, is sublime. And since it is, then so are we, for from the moment we are born until after we die we carry this sublimity within us.

FIGURE   **117**

INDEX